The Time Us
in the United
Beginning of the 21st Century

The Time Use of Mothers in the United States at the Beginning of the 21st Century

Rachel Connelly
Jean Kimmel

2010

W.E. Upjohn Institute for Employment Research
Kalamazoo, Michigan

Library of Congress Cataloging-in-Publication Data

Connelly, Rachel.
  The time use of mothers in the United States at the beginning of the 21st century /
Rachel Connelly, Jean Kimmel.
    p. cm.
  Includes bibliographical references and index.
  ISBN-13: 978-0-88099-368-5 (pbk. : alk. paper)
  ISBN-10: 0-88099-368-5 (pbk. : alk. paper)
  ISBN-13: 978-0-88099-369-2 (hardcover : alk. paper)
  ISBN-10: 0-88099-369-3 (hardcover : alk. paper)
  1. Mothers—Time management—United States—History—21st century. I. Kimmel,
Jean. II. Title.
  HQ759.C7245 2010
  306.874'30973090511—dc22
                          2010036017

© 2010
W.E. Upjohn Institute for Employment Research
300 S. Westnedge Avenue
Kalamazoo, Michigan 49007-4686

Cover design by Alcorn Publication Design.
Index prepared by Diane Worden.
Printed in the United States of America.
Printed on recycled paper.

To Michael, whose time has for so long been both a substitute and a complement to mine, and to our time-intensive children, Martin, Louis, Patrick, and William.

–RC

To David and Lizzie, whom I love very much. Your time-intensive travel soccer games are pure pleasure for me, except when Lizzie is in goal! Then not so much, but I am always proud. I couldn't have chosen a better way to spend my adult lifetime.

–JK

Contents

Figures

Tables

Acknowledgments

This study was generously supported by a grant from the W.E. Upjohn Institute for Employment Research. In addition, we received travel funds from the Bowdoin College Faculty Development Fund, the ATUS Early Results Conference, and the Institute for the Study of Labor (IZA). Bowdoin also provided funds for research assistants. Finally, both Bowdoin College and Western Michigan University provided resources for administrative support. We would like to thank Suzanne Bianchi, Nancy Folbre, Kimberly Fisher, John Fitzgerald, Daniel Hamermesh, Charlene Kalenkoski, Shelly Lundberg, Sabrina Pabilonia, David Ribar, Liana Sayer, Leslie Stratton, Jay Stewart, Anne Witte, Jayong Yoon, and all the participants at seminars at the ATUS Early Results Conference, the W.E. Upjohn Institute for Employment Research, IZA Topics Week, Brandeis University, and Rhodes College for their constructive comments and suggestions. We also benefited substantially from the comments of three anonymous referees for this manuscript and the anonymous referees for the related journal versions of Chapters 3, 4, and 5. Soon (Steve) Choi, Will Jacobs, Jonathan Rollins, Deweit Senbet, and Fei Tan all worked as research assistants on the project. Many thanks go to them for their efforts and data prowess. Elizabeth Weston carefully matched citations to bibliography and courageously did battle with Word for us. Thanks be to her. Results from the larger research project of which this monograph is a part have also been published in the *Journal of Human Resources*, the *Review of Economics of the Household*, and *Social Indicator Research*. We thank those journals for permission to publish overlapping material. Thanks finally to our kids for enabling us to speak with authority as mothers of children under age 13. Studying how other mothers use their time gives us insight into our own breathless lives. Despite the help of so many, the errors we make in our time allocation choices and in this monograph remain our own.

1
Introduction

One point of consensus regarding young children is that they consume a substantial portion of the time in a parent's day. Newborn babies must be cared for 24 hours a day. Yes, infants sleep, but the sleep is unpredictable and intermittent. As they age over those first few years, the sleep becomes more predictable, but they still need a caregiver's attention when awake. Young children still require a high level of adult attention. They can play by themselves for short periods of time, but the caregiver must be alert and on call. Where does this time devoted to young children come from?

Without a doubt, parents reallocate their time use to accommodate the caregiving demands of young children. They can also contract out some of that time to other family members or paid care providers. Mothers and fathers can take turns caring for children, or one can take primary responsibility for caregiving.

How families accommodate the time demands of young children has broad implications for overall time choices because time devoted to caregiving necessarily is time *not* devoted to other activities (with the exception of multitasking). Confronted with caregiving needs, we can work less in paid employment, study less, do less housework, have less leisure, or sleep less. If we pay for part of the caregiving, we will have less money for other goods and services. These choices are perfect examples of what economists mean when they talk about trade-offs. We trade off one time use for another, and very literally, we trade time for money.

This book focuses on the time use of mothers of preteenaged children in the United States from 2003 to 2006. We explore how mothers at the start of the twenty-first century are using their time in order to better understand their lives, the lives of their partners, and the lives of their children. Differences in the time choices American mothers make will have important implications for their own well-being and the well-being of family members. The study of maternal time use is hugely important because of the relationship between quality caregiving and

1

child well-being. Additionally, employers looking for new labor pools are also affected by the time use choices of mothers of young children because 60 percent of American mothers with young children are employed. Employers may want to cajole more mothers into the labor market or change the work hours for those women already in the labor market. The time choices of mothers in the United States also affect policymakers' thinking about things such as educational policy, the role that taxes play in the allocation of time between paid and unpaid activities, and possible expansion of publicly funded preschool.

The analysis provided in this book is possible because of the availability of a new, nationally representative data source that records the time use of persons in the United States over age 15. The American Time Use Survey (ATUS), which has been administered annually since 2003, provides large sample sizes and a full set of demographic characteristics, allowing social science researchers a better view of time use in the United States than has ever been available. Before the ATUS, researchers interested in time use of women in the United States had only a few limited time use surveys available.

BOOK OVERVIEW

In Chapter 2, we seek to answer the broad question of how mothers in the United States spend their time. More specifically, we examine the correlation between motherhood and leisure time, and we also consider whether mothers who work longer hours for pay spend less time with their children. Throughout the book, we distinguish between time use on weekends and weekdays because the two are substantively different. We also consider subgroups of mothers based on the age of their youngest child, marital status, and employment status. The age of a mother's youngest child is a particularly important determinant of time use due to the high demands young children place on caregivers' time. We do not distinguish between mothers, stepmothers, or adoptive mothers; instead, we define as mothers all those women coresiding with dependent children under the age of 13. Nor do we distinguish between married mothers with husbands present and cohabiting mothers; we refer to both groups as married mothers. Later in this chapter, we compare mothers' time use to that of women who are not mothers of young children, and we compare mothers' time use to that of fathers. Finally, we examine the time of day at which caregiving occurs.

Chapters 3, 4, and 5 provide three multivariate analyses of mothers' time uses as they relate to the caregiving needs of young children. In Chapter 3, we examine the role played by economic and demographic factors in mothers' time choices, and then ask the question, "Is caregiving time better characterized as household production or leisure?" While economic modeling clearly has moved beyond the labor/leisure dichotomy with the incorporation of household production time in these models, there is no consensus on where to place child caregiving in the trichotomy of labor, leisure, and home production. We allow caregiving to "speak for itself" by modeling four uses of a mother's time. The answer concerning the nature of caregiving is somewhat surprising: caregiving is not just a weighted average of leisure and home production; it is a wholly separate category of time use, neither fish nor fowl.

In Chapter 4, we examine more fully the role of husbands in mothers' time choices. Here, we extend the theoretical model of the mother's time use to include her husband's time. The result of these changes in the theoretical model leads us to include husband-specific variables in the estimation of the mother's nonmarket time uses. Specifically, we include three husband characteristics as critical factors affecting her time choices: his usual weekly employment hours, the relative wage (husband's wage divided by wife's wage), and his daily time in the same activity.[1] We find that relative wages are never significant determinants of the mother's time. The husband's weekly employment time affects her caregiving and home production time, and his time in the same activity seems to complement her home production time on the weekend. Additionally, her husband's caregiving time seems to complement her caregiving time on both weekdays and weekends. Finally, weekday leisure appears complementary while the effect of increased husband's leisure is negative on a mother's weekend leisure.

Chapter 5 looks beyond total time choices to examine questions related to the time of day of activities. Specifically, we ask the question, "How does the time of day that a mother is employed affect the amount of time spent with children throughout the day, in the morning, and in the evening?" We expect the time of day of employment to be important because children's time use is constrained by institutional structures such as school operating times, the availability of alternative caregivers, and the normal circadian rhythms of sleep. A consistent bimodal pattern of caregiving time shows that most child caregiving occurs in the morning and the evening. This is true regardless of the day of the week or children's ages. The consistency of caregiving time pushes us to ask the question, "What happens to caregiving time of mothers who are employed during those high (caregiving) demand morning and evening hours?" Do they just shift the time of caregiving earlier (or later), as Craig (2007) finds for Australian mothers, or do mothers employed in the early morning and evening provide less overall caregiving time? We find evidence of both the shifting of caregiving and the reduction of caregiving resulting from nonstandard work hours. Caregiving occurs earlier in the day for children of mothers who work early in the morning and later in the day for mothers who work later, but the mothers also provide less caregiving hours overall.

Chapter 6 concludes first with a review of the book's most important findings. Then, we relate general policy discussions to the specifics of these findings.

OVERVIEW OF THE ATUS

Our analysis relies on the recently released ATUS data to present a broad descriptive analysis of the current time allocation behaviors of mothers in the United States. Countries other than the United States have had ongoing time use surveys for many years, while for the United States, such surveys were administered infrequently, in 1965–1966 and 1975–1976, with smaller scale surveys in 1985–1986, 1992–1994, 1995, and 2000 (Hamermesh, Frazis, and Stewart 2005).[2] The sporadic administration of time use surveys in the United States, coupled with their small sample sizes, has greatly limited U.S. policy researchers. United States–based researchers have been calling for some time for a national commitment to time use surveys.[3] Finally, after nearly 10 years of development and planning, in 2003 the United States initiated the ATUS—an ongoing survey of time use (Horrigan and Herz 2004). The data from this first year of the ATUS were released in January 2005.

New samples of the ATUS are drawn annually from respondents of the monthly Current Population Survey (CPS) who are completing their stint in the survey sample. The linkage with the CPS, a large national survey, provides substantial additional information on the time survey respondent's household, though the CPS data are separated in time from the ATUS time diary collection by two to five months. Since time use changes very little from year to year, we use the first four years' worth of ATUS data as a single dataset. Controls for the year the data were collected are included in our analysis but are never statistically significant, which indicates that, at least at first blush, using the four years' worth of data as a single dataset is appropriate.

HISTORICAL TIME USE TRENDS OF MOTHERS

While the ATUS is the first nationally representative, large-scale time diary data collection in the United States, it builds off of 80 years' worth of small time diary studies in the United States and the substantial work of time researchers and time diary collection efforts in Western Europe, Canada, and Australia. This section reports on the work of several teams of researchers who have examined historical data to analyze changes in time use.

Bianchi, Robinson, and Milkie (2006)'s important book provides an in-depth portrait of time use within families in the United States, both in the present and over time. They describe the role played by gender, women's paid work, and family structure in the time allocation of both parents and their children. Their work serves as a starting point for our discussion of mothers' time use. Bianchi, Robinson, and Milkie note that over the past 40 years, despite rising female employment, maternal caregiving time has increased, while their time spent on housework has fallen. Mothers have accomplished this increased focus on family by forsaking some housework, multitasking, and including their children into their own leisure time (p. 2).

Trends in Home Production Time

Ramey and Francis (2006) and Ramey (2008) provide the longest historical examination of the available data, incorporating a series of small studies of housewives' time from the 1910s to the 1950s, as well as the nationally representative time surveys of 1965, 1975, 1985, and 1992.[4] The most surprising finding from their research is that the weekly hours of housework for full-time housewives did not decline from 1912 to the mid-1960s (Ramey and Francis 2006, p. 16). One might think that the diffusion of household technology (washing machines, vacuum cleaners, electrification, etc.) and a trend toward a smaller family size would have reduced home production hours, but changes in cleanliness standards and a reduction in the use of paid domestic labor seems to have countered any time gains from the new technology. Housework may be less physical than it was in the past, but the time devoted to housework did not change over those 50 years. Between the mid-1960s and the mid-1970s, there was a noticeable decline in home production time for nonworking women, which then leveled off until the present time (Ramey [2008, p. 23]; also observed by Robinson and Godbey [1999] and Aguiar and Hurst [2007]). Ramey and Francis show that employed women have spent less time on housework throughout the century, but that the proportion of the population of women they represent has, as we know, increased dramatically in the post–World War II era. Thus, looking at all women, hours of home production have declined largely as a result of changes in the percent of women in the labor force and the change in family size. Some of the decline in home production time is made up for by an increase in men's home production time, such that the average time devoted to home production by all prime-age individuals has not changed much over the long period studied by Ramey and Francis (2006) and by Ramey (2008).[5]

Bianchi et al. (2000) provide further support for the conclusion that the decline in housework since the mid-1960s has been driven by compositional changes. They focus on individuals, not just married couples, in order to determine the role that trends in marital status played in the decline in the gender gap in housework. They find a substantial decline in female housework along with an increase in male housework, resulting in a small shift in the gender division of labor within the household. They attribute this trend to compositional changes in the percent of women who are employed, but they also point to the importance played by delay in first marriage.[6]

Trends in Caregiving Time

There is a consensus among time researchers taking the long historical view that time reported as primarily engaged in child caregiving has increased over time. Ramey and Francis (2006) classify some child caregiving time as leisure and the rest as home production, making it difficult to examine the longest-term trend in caregiving.[7] Bryant and Zick (1996), using historical time use studies from 1924 (among the studies used by Ramey and Francis) and 1981, report that married women spent slightly more time on child caregiving in 1981 despite the significant decline in family size, implying that the time spent per child had increased. Ramey and Francis speculate that increased education and a growing social awareness of the benefits of parental interaction on child development may account for the increase in child care time per child.

While Sayer, Bianchi, and Robinson (2004) do not look back as far as Bryant and Zick (1996) or Ramey and Francis (2006), their careful historical look at the larger-scale time diary studies from the mid-1960s through 1998 focuses particularly on child caregiving time and its components.[8] They report that, overall, there has been an increase in child caregiving time from the mid-1960s to 1998 for both mothers and fathers. For mothers, the increased time pressures caused by increased employment time and a rise in single parenting seem to have been countered by reduced family size, older parenting, more parenting by choice (as opposed to as an unintended consequence of sex), greater concern over child safety and "changing cultural contexts of parenting and childhood" (p. 41). While employment alone would have reduced caregiving time and still does in the cross-section, trends in these other factors have outweighed the decline in child caregiving caused by increased employment, resulting in an increase in the total time reporting primary caregiving activities (Sayer, Bianchi, and Robinson 2004, Table 1, p. 18).

Bianchi, Wight, and Raley (2005) continue to focus on changes in caregiving time, but this is the first paper in this series of historical studies of caregiving time to include ATUS data. Their conclusion is that primary caregiving time has increased from 1975 to 2003. Between 1965 and 1975, child caregiving time of mothers with at least one child living in the household declined from 10 hours a week to 8½ hours. There was no change from 1975 to 1985, but then caregiving hours of mothers increased to 14.1 hours per week by 2003 (p. 13). Among caregiving hours, all of the increase is in the more interactive activities, such as playing with and reading to children. The caregiving time of employed mothers continues to be less than nonemployed mothers, but the caregiving time of an employed mother in 2000 was the same as that of a nonemployed mother in 1975. At the same time that mothers were increasing their hours of primary child caregiving, fathers were increasing theirs as well. By 2003, Bianchi, Wight, and Raley (2005) report an average of seven hours of paternal caregiving a week and a reduction in the ratio of mother's time to father's time (p. 13).

Trends in Leisure Time

With the observed reduction in home production time and accompanying increase in paid work time, what has happened to leisure time? According to Ramey and Francis (2006), per capita leisure essentially is unchanged from 1900 to 2000, with their per capita measure including the entire population. In contrast, Aguiar and Hurst (2007) document an increase in leisure from 1965 to the present for the working-age population (ages 21–65) who are neither in school nor retired, but this increase in leisure is largely among the group with low education levels.[9] Using a measure of "core leisure" that includes watching TV, socializing, participating in or watching sports, reading, hobby time, and other entertainment time, Aguiar and Hurst find an increase of 5.6 hours per week for men and 3.7 hours for women. These estimates control for changing demographics of the population from 1965 to the present.

Turning to leisure time for mothers, Bittman and Wajcman (2004) examine time diary data collected from 1981 to 1992 for 10 developed countries and find that employment and having young children have the largest influence in reducing adult leisure time (p. 182). Bianchi, Wight, and Raley (2005) present the leisure trends for mothers with at least one child under age 18 in the household. Excluding personal care time, leisure (they call it "free time") has declined about 3 hours a week, from 34.8 hours in 1965 to 31.6 in 2003. Their measure for 2000 is 31.8

hours, showing substantial continuity between the ATUS and the earlier University of Maryland data (Bianchi, Wight, and Raley 2000, Table 1). Thus, while total per capita leisure may have been constant and the leisure of the average working age person has increased, the leisure of mothers in the United States has declined slightly over the last 40 years as employment has increased and child caregiving time has also increased. These changes result in a growing feeling of time squeeze that Bittman and Wajcman (2004) find most likely to be reported by parents of young children.

POLICY IMPLICATIONS OF TIME USE STUDIES

To the extent that public policy affects incentives regarding time allocation, studies of time use using time diary data can help inform policy debates. Public policy relates to time use in two broad but inter-related ways: through its effect on the value of paid market work, such as taxing earned income or providing child care subsidies, and through family policies, such as the varying taxation for different family structures and the determination of child support and the support of human capital production.

Any increase in the marginal tax rate for earned income represents a decrease in the hourly wage received by the worker; thus, it is useful for policymakers to understand how this reduction in the market wage might affect time choices. When the market wage falls due to increased taxes, do individuals work more hours or fewer? Much evidence using traditional data sources exists to answer this question, but recent research has shown that estimates of labor supply responsiveness to wage changes tend to show much greater responsiveness when time diary data are used instead of the classical, retrospective measures of weekly hours worked. Additionally, estimates of wage elasticities might be biased by ignoring other time uses such as household production or leisure (Apps 2005). We contribute to the stock of knowledge in this policy area by estimating expanded models of time use that consider jointly several aggregate time uses, including paid work.

In addition to the effect of wage changes on paid work efforts, policymakers should also be interested in knowing the effect that such policies have on other time uses. For example, what is the relationship between higher market wages and time spent with children? There is some evidence that higher-educated individuals devote more time to primary caregiving, but to date, the analyses have not included a full set of time uses to facilitate understanding of the trade-offs associated with transferring time from one activity to another.[10] We address this question in our expanded model of time use by focusing on a measure of the wage that incorporates the mother's education as well as other measures of productivity, and we use appropriate statistical methodologies that adjust for other factors important to time use decision making.

Many policies have implications for family structure and family decision making. For example, policies that affect the individual's wage may affect the division of unpaid household labor within a household. The way household labor is divided within couples is important because of issues concerning equality of this unpaid time burden and the degree to which spousal support in housework facilitates success in employment. Additionally, public policies determine the size of child support payments based on the income requirements of raising a child but without consideration for unpaid household production and caregiving time requirements.

Perhaps the most important "output" produced in unpaid household production is "quality" children who grow up to become productive members of society.[11] As is well established, parental time with children affects child development (see, for example, National Institute of Child Health and Human Development Early Child Care Research Network [1994]). Thus, any public policy that affects time devoted to child caregiving will have implications for our nation's future workforce productivity. According to Smeeding and Marchand (2004), "Parental time devoted to children lays the foundation for future acquisition of formal human capital" (p. 30). Ramey and Ramey (2008) argue that a substantial increase in parental caregiving time by college-educated parents in the United States is motivated by the goal of increasing the college admission prospects of their children. Growing inequality of income seems to be coupled with growing inequality of caregiving time, which further increases the hurdles low-income children face in attaining parity in educational attainment with children from higher-income homes. We are interested in whether public policy aggravates or helps mitigate these time and money gaps.

Public policy can also have some effect on the timing of activities across the day. Time use data can be used to analyze when activities occur during the day and how policy might affect this timing. As explained by Hamermesh and Pfann (2005), "When we do things matters . . . People develop habits that allow them to economize on their timing of activities, just as they develop patterns of goods consumption, and time use that maximizes their satisfaction at a point in time and over their lifetimes" (p. 3). For example, local laws concerning store hours or "Blue Laws" that prohibit the sale of alcohol on Sundays have implications for individuals' ability to maximize utility by choosing fully the timing of activities across a day and a week (Jacobsen and Kooreman 2005). The hours that public schools are open and the annual academic calendar can also be seen as public policies that affect parents' caregiving.

Finally, policymakers are interested in measuring the value of unpaid household work for a variety of purposes. In fact, according to Joyce and Stewart (1999), "Perhaps the most fundamental application of time-use data would be to provide nationally representative estimates of the amount of time that Americans spend in various activities" (p. 1). First, such measures can facilitate measurement of well-being as household-produced goods are consumed jointly with purchased goods. Second, the ability to measure and, thus, value unpaid work can contribute to improvement in measures of national output, which could give us a better understanding of national productivity and its trend over time.

Notes

1. Spousal time use is not observed directly in the ATUS. In Chapter 4, we propose a "data construction" strategy.
2. For years, labor economics research in numerous other countries (including Australia, Canada, Germany, Israel, Korea, the United Kingdom) have used national time use survey data to investigate topics such as household production technologies (Gronau and Hamermesh 2006) and parental time inputs in children (Kalenkoski, Ribar, and Stratton 2005; Robinson and Godbey 1997; Sandberg and Hofferth 2001). Time use studies can also be used be to generate alternative measures of hours of market work (Frazis and Stewart 2004; Klevmarken 2004; Robinson and Bostrom 1994) and to examine the time of day activities take place (Hamermesh 1999; Jacobsen and Kooreman 2005). Works that have tracked

U.S. time use trends include Robinson and Godbey (1999) and, for parents, Bianchi, Robinson, and Milkie (2006).

3. The National Survey of Families and Households and the Panel Survey of Income Dynamics collect very limited time use information. For a comparison among these two surveys and the ATUS, see Winkler (2002).

4. These latter four surveys have been carefully standardized and combined to create the American Heritage Time Use Study (AHTUS) by the Centre of Time Use Research at the Institute for Social and Economic Research at the University of Essex and analyzed by Fisher et al. (2006), among others.

5. Note that Bryant and Zick (1996) shows a one-hour decline in daily household work for married mothers for this same period.

6. Vanek (1974) finds that housework did not decline in the 1960s relative to the 1920s. Note, however, that the 1920s sample contained rural women while the 1960s sample was comprised of urban women.

7. Ramey and Francis (2006) follow Aguiar and Hurst's (2007) lead and classify talking to, playing with, and reading to children as leisure.

8. Sayer, Bianchi, and Robinson (2004) compare the same 1965, 1975, 1985 surveys that appear in the AHTUS plus a University of Maryland survey from 1998, while Bianchi, Wight, and Raley (2005) compare 1965, 1975, 1985, 1995, 1998, 2000 surveys and the first year of the ATUS, 2003.

9. Aguiar and Hurst (2007 and 2008) use data from 1965, 1985, and the ATUS of 2003–2005.

10. For an early paper in this vein, see Hill and Stafford (1974).

11. We use the word quality first popularized by Gary Becker, who wrote extensively about the quality-quantity trade-off for children. According to Becker, quality children simply means they receive more inputs. Our definition of quality children are children who are emotionally healthy, physically cared for, and happy. In most cases, more inputs will lead to quality children, especially if one includes parental time as an input.

2
A Descriptive Look at Mothers' Time Use

In the previous chapter, we briefly described the ATUS data. In this chapter, we describe the data collection effort in much more detail. Then, we begin to explore the data by looking at the time use of mothers in the United States. We consider how this time use varies by weekend versus weekday, the age of the children, and marital and employment status. We also include a time use comparison of mothers versus non-mothers, and mothers versus fathers. Our focus is mainly on primary caregiving time. We describe what is included in this category and consider alternative measures of caregiving also available in the data.

FURTHER DESCRIPTION OF THE ATUS

The ATUS provides detailed information about time use, and the accompanying CPS file provides extensive demographic and labor market information. The ATUS collects one 24-hour time diary per selected household. A day of the week and an adult (household member above 15 years of age) are randomly assigned to a selected household. Weekend days are oversampled such that about one-half of the diary days are from Saturday or Sunday and the other half are from a weekday. We include weekday holidays with weekend days, as there are few holidays and they appear in preliminary analysis much more like weekends than weekdays.

Telephone interviewers call on the day after the chosen survey day of the week and ask the respondent to recall what he or she was doing the previous day beginning at 4 a.m. and concluding with 4 a.m. the day of the interview. Responses are categorized into more than 300 different detailed time categories with 17 main categories.[1] We aggregate these detailed categories into five composite time use categories: 1) paid work, 2) leisure, 3) unpaid home production, 4) child caregiving, and

5) all other activities.[2] We believe that these five aggregate categories represent fundamentally different uses of time, each yielding utility and disutility in distinctive ways.

Paid work time mainly contributes to well-being through increased income (resulting from increased work hours or an increase in the hourly wage), which eases the family's budget constraint. Leisure contributes to well-being directly via the process of engaging in the activity. We define leisure as "active leisure," similar to Aguiar and Hurst (2007). Home production time contributes to well-being mostly through the commodities that are produced, though a few of the activities may also be enjoyable. (The same can be said, however, about employment time.) Caregiving provides a mix of outputs, direct well-being, like leisure (loving children or enjoying spending time with children), indirect production commodities, like home production (clean children), and a large dose of investment toward future direct utility and production commodities (loving and educated adult children). Finally, the Other category is mainly investment, including sleep as investment into current productivity, and education and work-related investments as investments in future productivity. Appendix A gives full details showing how we collapse the many ATUS time uses into our five composite categories.

From the full ATUS sample, we extract all the women aged 18–60 with at least one child under age 13 in the household. All of the analysis in the book focuses on this population group, whom we call "mothers." For the descriptive discussions in this chapter, we also construct a sample whom we refer to as "nonmothers." Nonmothers include women aged 18–60 who have no children under age 13 in the household. Thus, nonmothers include some mothers whose youngest child is a teenager and women who have no children. Finally, we construct a sample of "fathers" that parallels the sample of mothers except that we included an upper age limit of 65, since men tend to be slightly older than women when their children are born.

The focus of this book is on maternal caregiving, thus our definition of caregiving requires careful explanation. We use "primary caregiving" or just "caregiving time" to refer to caregiving reported by the mothers or fathers as the primary activity. Primary caregiving is the measure of caregiving that we rely on for the bulk of this chapter as well as for our empirical work presented in Chapters 3, 4, and 5.

According to the ATUS Coding Rules' discussion of primary child care reproduced in Appendix B, "Determining when an activity should be coded as child care can be difficult. Neither the presence of a child during the respondent's activity nor a child's participation in the respondent's activity is sufficient alone to code the activity as child care . . . When the respondent is directly watching or interacting with a child only, or accompanying a child to an activity that has no purpose outside the child, then code as child care" (Bureau of Labor Statistics [BLS] 2008a, p. 9).

Beyond the definition of primary caregiving, other important issues with the ATUS are the response rate and the fact that there is only one time diary collected per household for only a single 24-hour period. Perhaps the most important concern is the relatively low response rate for the ATUS. The response for the ATUS is under 60 percent, which is much lower than the CPS response rate but still high relative to other time diary collection efforts (Abraham, Maitland, and Bianchi 2006, p. 677). Inadequate survey response can bias the findings produced by the data if survey responders are qualitatively different from survey nonresponders in critical ways. To address this concern, Abraham, Maitland, and Bianchi (2006) examine the source of the low response rate and explain that it can arise from the failure to achieve initial contact with a potential survey responder, or once contacted, a refusal to participate in the survey. Abraham, Maitland, and Bianchi explain that in the ATUS, the bulk of the low survey response is due to contact failure, which appears to be somewhat randomly distributed across the population.

A second source of low survey response is that, once contacted, potential respondents may refuse to participate in the survey. Although there was some concern that individuals who are busy with their lives might be less likely to participate in the survey (thereby producing a large bias in time use measures that would be obtained from such tarnished data), this does not seem to be a significant concern with the ATUS (Abraham, Maitland, and Bianchi 2006). The critical way that nonresponders differ is via their connection to community; that is, those not contacted appear to be less connected to community. This fact may produce bias in studies that focus on community connection characteristics, such as studies of volunteerism. In fact, research has shown that studies of volunteerism using the ATUS suffer from the fact that those individuals most likely to volunteer are also particularly more likely to agree to participate in the survey in the first place. (Abraham, Helms, and Presser 2009).[3]

A second set of data concerns relates to the structure of the ATUS; specifically, that the time diaries are collected for only one adult per household and for only a single 24-hour period. Thus, issues surrounding the division of unpaid household labor in a given household or the synchronization of couples' leisure are difficult to examine. We present a methodology in Chapter 4 for overcoming this data insufficiency. The second component of this concern is the fact that the time diary data reflect only a single 24-hour period. To the extent that this single day is randomly selected, estimation methods that reflect averages across many individuals may adjust appropriately for this data drawback. Other surveys (such as the German Time Use Survey) collect diaries for more than a single day to avoid this problem.[4]

The issue of how much information is collected relates to the response rate concerns discussed earlier. Collecting time diaries from all members of a household would increase costs and reduce response rates. So too would collecting more than one 24-hour time diary. The BLS/census administrators of the ATUS have had to make choices among sample size, response rates, and amount of information collected. The choice to collect a single 24-hour time diary increases response rates and allows for larger sample sizes.

MOTHERS' TIME USE ON A TYPICAL DAY

Figure 2.1 shows the breakdown of mothers' time on a weekday into our five categories, while Figure 2.2 shows the breakdown of time for these mothers on weekends. On both weekdays and weekends, the category to which mothers devote the most time is Other since it is the category that includes sleep. It is interesting to note that this category is larger on weekends, indicating that weekends may be more restful than weekdays. On weekdays, mothers spend 10 percent of their time in child caregiving activities, 20 percent in leisure, 14 percent on home production, and 15 percent on paid employment. Weekends differ with paid work time reduced substantially and leisure time increased. How-

Figure 2.1 Weekday Time Use of All Mothers

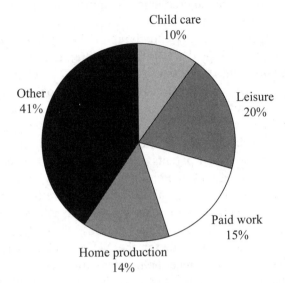

Figure 2.2 Weekend Time Use of All Mothers

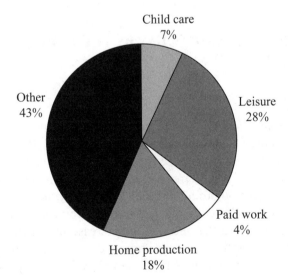

ever, weekends also appear to serve as opportunities to be productive around the house as home production is significantly increased from 14 to 18 percent on weekends.

What happens to primary caregiving on the weekend? Mothers are not engaged in much paid work, their children are not in school, yet caregiving falls from 10 percent of total time to 7 percent of total time. Caregiving, as described previously, is composed of primary activities focused on children. Purely supervisory time may not be included as caregiving time, but rather as the activity in which one is engaged while supervising the children. In addition, the rules of coding presented in Appendix B show that if parents are participating together in a recreational activity along with the children, the activity may be classified as recreation, not child care. This situation is more likely to occur on weekends, when men's employment time is also substantially reduced (see Figures 2.14b and 2.14d on pp. 37–38). Thus, it seems that the caregiving activities as recorded in the ATUS (and probably in previous time diaries as well, since the numbers track fairly well across all the previous time diary collections, as shown in Bianchi, Wight, and Raley [2005]) are mainly structured time devoted to caregiving, getting the children up and ready for the day, homework time, reading a book together, and getting them ready for bed.[5]

TIME USE ON A TYPICAL DAY BY THE AGE OF THE YOUNGEST CHILD

Figures 2.3 and 2.4 compare an average weekday for mothers whose youngest child is 0–5 and 6–12, respectively. As expected, mothers of preschoolers devote substantially more of their daily time to primary caregiving (13 percent for these mothers versus 7 percent for mothers of older children). This difference is statistically significant at the 1 percent level. Household production and "other" time are similar for these two groups of mothers (though the small differences are statistically significant), implying that most of the increase in primary caregiving for mothers of preschoolers comes from reduced leisure and paid work. Most of the difference comes from the reduced weekday employment time of mothers with the youngest children, but these mothers also have

Figure 2.3 Weekday Time Use of Mothers of Children Aged 0–5

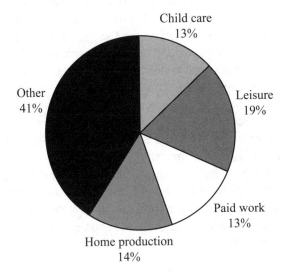

Figure 2.4 Weekday Time Use of Mothers of Children Aged 6–12

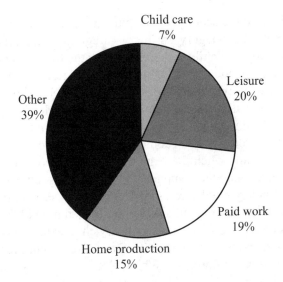

slightly less leisure time as well. These differences are both statistically significant. Interestingly, the leisure time they do have is largely in the presence of children, but that is also true for all mothers. The percent of leisure time on a weekday in which the mother is alone varies from 15 percent to 22 percent, respectively, for mothers with the youngest children and mothers whose youngest child is 6–12. On weekends, only 8 percent of a mother's leisure time is spent alone when her youngest child is 0–5, compared to 13 percent when her youngest child is 6–12. All of these differences are significant at the 1 percent level.[6]

As shown in Figures 2.5 and 2.6, on weekends, paid work time is mostly unchanged when comparing the five categories of aggregated time use of mothers whose youngest child is 0–5 and 6–12, though the differences are significant at the 1 percent level. Since primary caregiving is 5 percentage points more for mothers with preschoolers, this significantly increased caregiving time must come from other time, home production, and leisure categories.

DESCRIPTIVE EVIDENCE CONCERNING ALTERNATIVE CAREGIVING MEASURES

In addition to the set of primary time use activities we have aggregated to create the category "primary caregiving," the ATUS probed further on the topic of child caregiving. After the full 24-hour diary was collected, all respondents with children under age 13 in the household were asked during which activities did they have a child "under their care." They were also asked when the first child under 13 woke up and when the last child under 13 went to sleep. This period of time during which children were awake becomes the potential secondary child care time measure. Time when the respondent is engaged in primary caregiving and time when the respondent is asleep are subtracted from this potential secondary child care time. Any potential secondary child care time in which the respondent said he or she had a child "under his or her care" is then categorized as "secondary child care." This secondary child care is characterized by the ATUS as "care for children under age 13 that is done while doing something else as a primary activity, such as cooking dinner" (BLS 2008b, p. 34). One must be especially careful

Figure 2.5 Weekend Time Use of Mothers of Children Aged 0–5

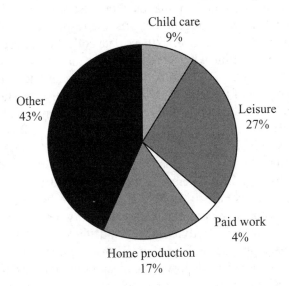

Figure 2.6 Weekend Time Use of Mothers of Children Aged 6–12

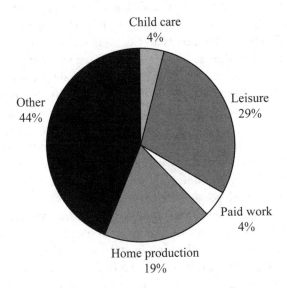

with the terminology "secondary child care," since the ATUS definition just described is different from that used in most other time diary data. In many time diary data collection efforts, the respondent is allowed to report doing two things at once. In those data collection efforts, secondary child care is the time when caregiving is recorded as the secondary activity. The ATUS chose not to collect any secondary activities in the time diary portion of the survey and instead added the questions about "in your care" after the formal diary collection was completed. Bianchi, Wight, and Raley (2005) show that while the primary child caregiving in the 2000 National Survey of Parents (NSP) and the 2003 ATUS data are very similar, the level of secondary child care reported in the ATUS is substantially higher: mothers of children under 13 report 1 hour on average of secondary care in the NSP and 6.9 in the ATUS (Table 5).

Because secondary care excludes the time when child care was reported as the primary activity, one could think of total caregiving time as primary plus secondary time.[7] However, this total caregiving time may be too broad a category to be meaningful in terms of decision making analysis since many mothers included all time between waking and sleeping of the child as time when the child was under their care.

An alternative measure of total caregiving time is also possible with the ATUS because during the diary collection portion of the survey, the respondents are asked, in addition to what they were doing at each moment of the day, with whom they were performing the activity.[8] From the "with whom" data, one can calculate the time mothers spend in the presence of children. As one would imagine, caregiving time measured as time with children is substantially greater than the time in which parents report child care as the primary activity. We report time with children exclusive of primary caregiving time as an alternative measure of secondary caregiving, and time with children plus primary caregiving time as our preferred measure of total caregiving time.

Figure 2.7 compares primary caregiving time, time with children, and secondary caregiving time for mothers for weekdays and weekends. The figure should assuage the concern some might have felt about caregiving time being less on weekends. Primary caregiving time is less on the weekends (102 minutes on average compared to 149 minutes on a weekday), but both time with children and secondary caregiving time are greater on the weekends. Overall, we have argued that secondary care is a broader measure of caregiving than time with children, and

Figure 2.7 Comparison of Time Spent Primary Caregiving, Time with Children, and Secondary Caregiving for All Mothers

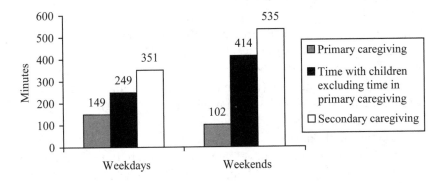

the greater number of minutes of secondary care compared to time with children on both weekdays and weekends supports that characterization.[9] Which measure one chooses to use depends, in part, on the context of the caregiving discussion. If, for example, one were interested in the effect of time investments in children on child outcomes, then primary or maybe time with children measures would be best. If, on the other hand, one were interested in exploring gendered differences in leisure time (as in Bittman and Wajcman [2004]), then secondary child care might be a better measure of constrained time (as opposed to free time or leisure). Lamb, Pleck, and Charnov (1985) divide parenting into three components: 1) interaction, 2) availability, and 3) responsibility. The primary child care time in the ATUS is mostly interaction time, though it also includes the time parents spend making child care arrangements, which could be considered in the responsibility category. Availability could be thought of as either time with children or time when the child is in your care. Lamb, Pleck, and Charnov's (1985) last category, responsibility, is even broader, since making dinner for the children and earning money to pay for the dinner ingredients would also be included. Once we include these time uses, all time other than sleep and leisure time away from children would have to be included. Folbre et al. (2005) argue that time with children should be included in measures of caregiving, as it surely acts as a constraint to mothers' behavior, and one would have to pay someone to perform these services. However, Bianchi, Wight, and Raley (2005) argue that when all time is included, the measure ceases to be meaningful "other than to indicate that parents almost always feel responsible for their children" (p. 21).[10]

Figures 2.8 and 2.9 present the weekday and weekend pictures of total caregiving time, which is the sum of primary caregiving and time with children. These figures show that total caregiving time is 467 minutes (almost 8 hours) on weekdays for mothers with a child aged 0–5 and 557 minutes (9¼ hours) on weekends. Total caregiving time is reduced to 311 minutes (6 hours) on weekdays for mothers whose youngest child is 6–12 and 457 on weekends (7½ hours).

In these figures we have divided primary caregiving time into developmental child care time and other primary child care activities. Included in the measure of developmental child care time is time spent talking and playing with children, reading to and helping with homework, arts and crafts, and homeschooling. Other primary child care activities are mainly the physical care of children, but also time making child care arrangements and travel time related to caregiving. Using the levels of time shown in Figures 2.8 and 2.9, we can derive the proportion of developmental time to all primary caregiving time. These proportions are provided in Table 2.1. One might expect the proportion of developmental time to total primary caregiving time to increase with the age of the child as they have more homework and are more capable of bathing and dressing themselves, but Table 2.1 shows just the opposite—the proportion of primary caregiving time that is developmental

Figure 2.8 Mothers' Time Spent on Types of Caregiving, by Age of the Youngest Child, on Weekdays

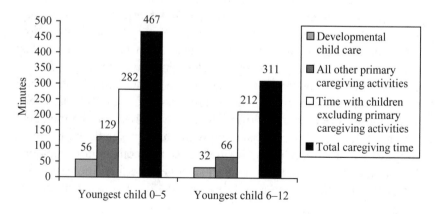

Figure 2.9 Mothers' Time Spent on Types of Caregiving, by Age of the Youngest Child, on Weekends

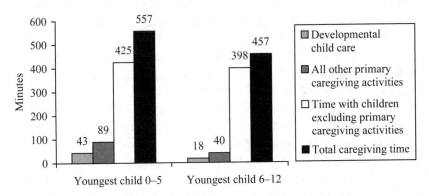

significantly declines as the child ages. In addition, the proportion is significantly reduced on weekends compared to weekdays.

TIME USE DIFFERENCES BY MARITAL STATUS

Thus far, we have not distinguished between mothers except by the age of their youngest child and weekday versus weekend diary collection. In this section we consider differences in mothers' time use by their marital status, and in the next section we consider differences in mothers' time use by their employment status.[11] Of course, there may be correlations between these two characteristics as well, but we will

Table 2.1 Proportion of Mothers' Primary Caregiving Time That Is Developmental

	Weekdays	Weekends	Significant difference
Youngest child aged 0–5	41.4	34.4	***
Youngest child aged 6–12	37.3	29.6	***
Significant difference	***	***	

NOTE: Asterisks based on t-tests comparing the proportions. ***indicates that the proportions are different at the 0.01 level.

leave that for the multivariate analyses in the following chapters. Figure 2.10 compares the weekday and weekend, primary caregiving time and time with children excluding primary caregiving time for married and unmarried mothers of children under the age of 13. Unmarried mothers have significantly lower caregiving time in all categories. Table 2.2 fills in some detail by comparing the caregiving minutes of married and unmarried mothers by the age of their youngest children and providing the results of the t-tests of mean minutes. In almost every category, married mothers devote significantly more time to child caregiving than unmarried mothers. For time spent with 6–12-year-olds excluding primary caregiving time, the difference is not significant across marital status. The lower numbers overall may be the result of the time crunch faced by unmarried mothers, who may have no one with whom to trade time. There are other possibilities as well because of correlations between marital status, education, employment, etc.

Table 2.3 shows the percent of time in each of the five aggregated time use categories for married and unmarried mothers by the age of the youngest child and weekday versus weekend. The differences between married and unmarried caregiving time are not significant once we control for the age of the youngest child and the day of week. This table shows that unmarried women spend less of their time in home produc-

Figure 2.10 Mothers' Caregiving Time, by Marital Status, for Weekdays and Weekends

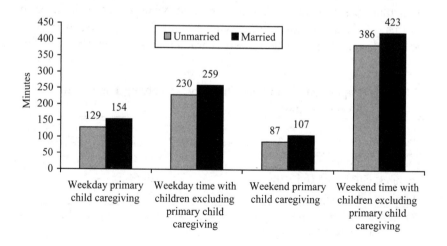

tion in all cases. Employment time is greater for unmarried mothers of very young children on weekends. In the next section we examine this bivariate relationship between employment status and caregiving time.

TIME USE DIFFERENCES BY EMPLOYMENT STATUS

As we report in Chapter 1, one of the surprises in the historical comparison of time use is that primary child caregiving time has increased over the last 40 years. The initial expectation was that caregiving time would have declined during this era of revolutionary increases in women's labor force participation, particularly for mothers of young children. Since time is always scarce, the increase in employment time was expected to come from caregiving time as well as from leisure and home production. Research by Bianchi, Wight, and Raley (2005) and Sayer, Bianchi, and Robinson (2004) has shown that while "time with children" has declined over this period, countervailing changes in family size, family income levels, safety concerns, and perhaps even employed mothers' maternal guilt about time away from their children, together have led to a net increase in primary caregiving time.[12] Fisher's (2005) work shows that this increase can be seen in all subcategories of caregiving with the exception of reading to and talking with children, which declines in the years of ATUS data collection. Fisher argues that the decline in reading to and talking with children is probably due to these activities being reported as secondary activities performed in conjunction with housework or travel time, and thus missed by the ATUS since it collects only primary activities.

The overall increase in primary caregiving over time is consistent with differentials in caregiving time by employment status. It is still the case that more time in one activity must mean less time in another activity, and Figure 2.11 shows that more time in employment is significantly related to less primary caregiving time on both weekdays and weekends. The differences in caregiving time between mothers employed 35 or more hours per week and nonworking mothers are about 1½ hours of care per weekday and about half an hour more of care per weekend day, which sums to a weekly difference of about 8½ hours. While this 8½ hour difference in primary maternal caregiving is substantial, this

Table 2.2 Caregiving Minutes by Marital Status, Age of Youngest Child, and Weekdays versus Weekends

	Weekdays		Significant	Weekends		Significant
	Married	Unmarried	difference	Married	Unmarried	difference
Primary caregiving						
Youngest child aged 0–5	191	165	***	137	115	***
Youngest child aged 6–12	102	90	**	61	51	**
Time with children excluding primary caregiving						
Youngest child aged 0–5	290	252	***	430	407	**
Youngest child aged 6–12	215	206	***	412	359	***

NOTE: Asterisks represent results of t-test of means across marital status. **significant at the 0.05 level; ***significant at the 0.01 level.

Table 2.3 Percent of Mothers' Time by Marital Status, Age of Youngest Child, and Weekdays versus Weekends

	Youngest child aged 0–5			Youngest child aged 6–12		
	Weekday		Significant difference	Weekday		Significant difference
	Married	Unmarried		Married	Unmarried	
Child care	13	12		7	6	
Leisure	18	19		20	21	
Paid work	13	14		19	18	
Home production	15	11	**	15	12	*
Other	40	44	*	39	42	
	Weekend			Weekend		
	Married	Unmarried		Married	Unmarried	
Child care	10	8		4	4	
Leisure	27	27		29	29	
Paid work	3	5	**	4	5	
Home production	18	14	*	20	16	*
Other	43	46		43	46	

NOTE: Asterisks represent results of t-test of proportions across marital status. *significant at the 0.10 level; **significant at the 0.05 level.

**Figure 2.11 Mothers' Primary Child Caregiving Time, by Weekly
Employment Status**

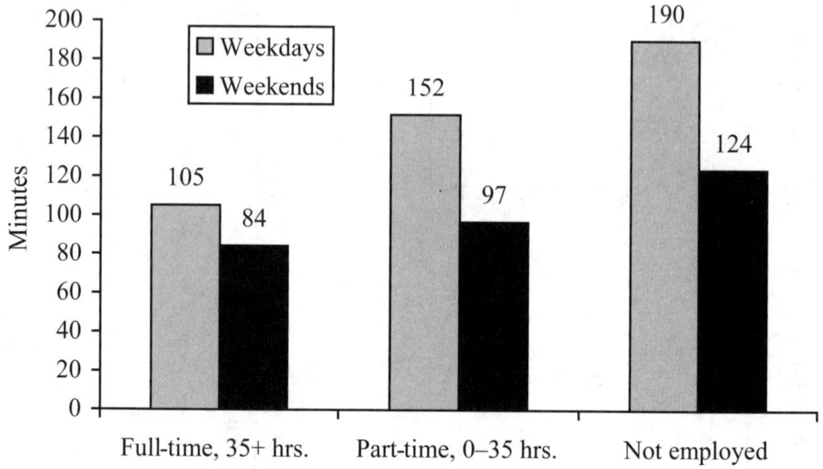

decline in primary caregiving is much less than the average hours of paid work for full-time employed mothers. Clearly, much employment time is drawn from activities other than primary caregiving.[13]

Figures 2.12a–d show the full distribution of time for full-time employed mothers and nonemployed mothers on weekdays and weekends.[14] On weekdays, nonemployed mothers spend significantly more time in each of the four remaining categories of time, only marginally so for "other" time, but on weekends, the two groups of mothers are similar in their home production and "other" time. Caregiving time and leisure are higher for nonemployed mothers than employed mothers on weekends, but the differences between the two groups are less than on weekdays.

Because employment status is related to the age of the youngest child, Figure 2.13a explores the difference in primary caregiving time and total caregiving time by employment status for mothers of children 0–5, and Figure 2.13b shows the same relationships for mothers whose youngest child is 6–12 years of age. What is interesting here is how similar the weekend times are among women across employment states. This is true especially for the primary child caregiving time of mothers whose youngest child is school-aged. Part-time employed mothers and nonemployed mothers spend about an hour in primary caregiving activ-

Figure 2.12a Weekday Distribution of Time for Full-Time Employed Mothers

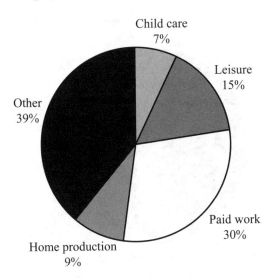

Figure 2.12b Weekday Distribution of Time for Nonemployed Mothers

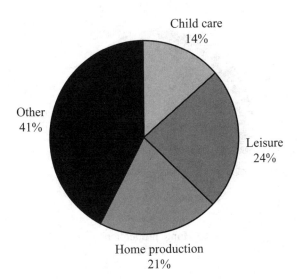

**Figure 2.12c Weekend Distribution of Time for Full-Time
Employed Mothers**

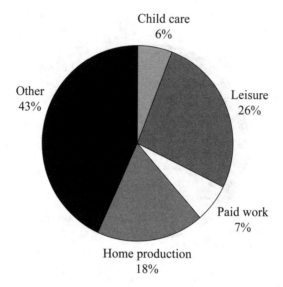

Figure 2.12d Weekend Distribution of Time for Nonemployed Mothers

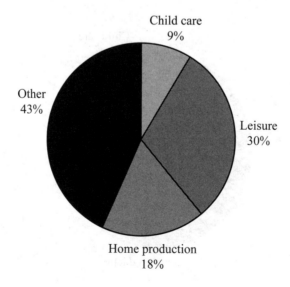

Figure 2.13a Primary and Total Caregiving Time for Mothers Whose Youngest Child is 0–5

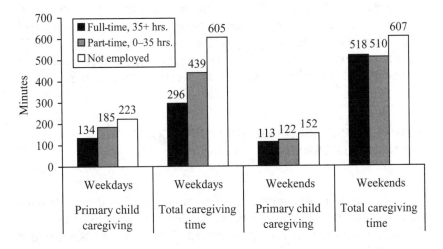

Figure 2.13b Primary and Total Caregiving Time for Mothers Whose Youngest Child is 6–12

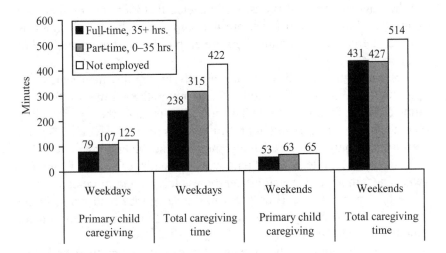

ities with their school-aged children on weekend days, while full-time employed mothers spend just 10 minutes less time.[15] Most employment time does take place on weekdays, although in Chapter 3 we show that mothers with preschool-aged children have more weekend employment hours than other mothers. It may be the case that some working mothers, particularly those working part time, adjust their work schedules so that another family member is available to care for their young children.

TIME USE PATTERNS OF MOTHERS COMPARED TO NONMOTHERS

In this section we compare the daily time use of mothers with nonmothers. Recall that nonmothers are defined as women of comparable age to mothers but without preteenaged children in the household.[16] Nonmothers in our sample are on average older—the mean age of nonmothers is 41 years of age compared to 34 for mothers—and they are less likely to be married or cohabiting—54 percent of the nonmothers are married compared to 76 percent of the mothers. Given the differences in their age and marital status, we expected that more nonmothers are employed full time and fewer are not employed. The ATUS confirms this: 56 percent of the nonmothers are employed full time compared to 42 percent of the mothers.

Because time use differs substantially by employment status, we present the comparison of mothers' and nonmothers' time use for full-time employed women. Table 2.4 shows that most of the 7 percent difference in primary caregiving time of mothers on weekdays comes from leisure with only a 1 percentage point difference in employment hours. The differences in leisure and paid work are statistically significant. On weekends, mothers have significantly less leisure and more caregiving time than nonmothers. Time spent in the categories paid work, home production, and other are not significantly different between mothers and nonmothers on weekends.

Table 2.5 compares the time use of nonemployed mothers and nonemployed nonmothers on both weekdays and weekends. Nonemployed mothers spent a substantial amount of their time in primary caregiving. Nonemployed nonmothers spent significantly more time in leisure and

Table 2.4 Percent of Time Use by Full-Time Employed Mothers and Nonmothers, Weekdays and Weekends

	Weekdays		Significant difference	Weekends		Significant difference
	Non-mothers	Mothers		Non-mothers	Mothers	
Child care	0	7	***	0	6	***
Leisure	19	15	***	31	26	***
Paid work	31	30		7	7	
Household production	9	9		17	18	
Other	40	39		44	43	

NOTE: Sample comprises only mothers and nonmothers (only women), aged 60 years or younger, of children aged 0–12 years old. Asterisks represent results of t-test of proportions across mother status. ***significant at the 0.01 level.

Table 2.5 Percent of Time Use by Nonemployed Mothers and Nonmothers, Weekdays and Weekends

	Weekdays		Significant difference	Weekends		Significant difference
	Non-mothers	Mothers		Non-mothers	Mothers	
Child care	0	14	***	0	9	***
Leisure	32	24	***	37	30	***
Household production	20	21		16	18	
Other	48	42	***	46	43	*

NOTE: Sample comprises only mothers and nonmothers (only women), aged 60 years or younger, of children aged 0–12 years old. Asterisks represent results of t-test of proportions across mother status. *significant at the 0.10 level; ***significant at the 0.01 level.

other activities. Interestingly, their home production is not significantly different on either weekdays or weekends.

TIME USE PATTERNS OF MOTHERS COMPARED TO FATHERS

The review of the historical data on time use shows that fathers' caregiving time has increased substantially over the last 40 years, though fathers' caregiving time started from a very low level and remains considerably less than the caregiving time of mothers. Our analysis shows that fathers now devote about 5 percent of their time to caregiving. Figures 2.14a–d show the direct comparison of mothers and fathers on weekdays and weekends. On weekdays, mothers spend 10 percent of their time on primary caregiving while fathers spend 4 percent. Fathers increase their time in child caregiving to 5 percent on weekends, while mothers decrease their time in caregiving to 7 percent on weekends. Fathers and mothers enjoy very similar levels of leisure on the weekdays (no significant difference), but on weekends, when fathers' paid employment hours have been substantially reduced, fathers devote a third of their time to leisure compared to mothers' 28 percent—that translates into a statistically significant difference of more than an hour.

Like mothers, fathers' caregiving time is reduced as the youngest child ages. Table 2.6 shows mothers' and fathers' primary caregiving time and time with children by weekdays and weekends and by the age of their youngest child. On weekdays, fathers' primary child caregiving time falls less quickly as the age of the youngest child increases than mothers', such that the ratio of mothers' time to fathers' time declines. On weekends, the decline in primary caregiving time by age of the youngest child is more similar for mothers and fathers such that the ratio between their time is essentially constant at 1.5 to 1. In addition, on weekends, time inputs of mothers and fathers are more similar, especially when we consider total caregiving time. Sayer, Bianchi, and Robinson (2004) report very similar ratios of caregiving time for mothers and fathers from their 1998 survey, and show that the ratio of married mothers' to married fathers' primary caregiving time has declined dramatically over the 30 years for which they have data (p. 23).

Figure 2.14a Weekday Time Use of All Mothers

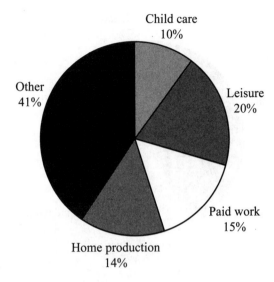

Figure 2.14b Weekday Time Use of All Fathers

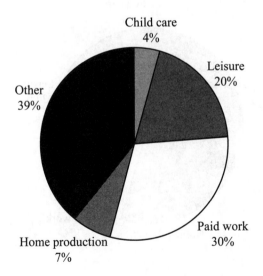

Figure 2.14c Weekend Time Use of All Mothers

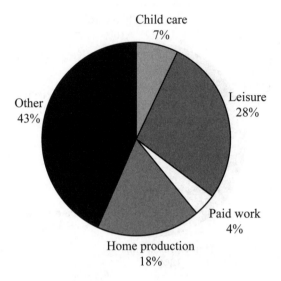

Figure 2.14d Weekend Time Use of All Fathers

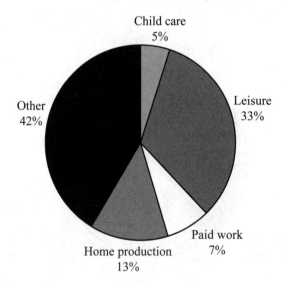

Table 2.6 Mothers' and Fathers' Primary Caregiving Time and Total Caregiving Time, by Age of Youngest Child and Weekdays versus Weekends

	Mother		Father		Ratio of mothers' to fathers' time when youngest child is 0–5	Ratio of mothers' to fathers' time when youngest child is 6–12
	Youngest child is 0–5	Youngest child is 6–12	Youngest child is 0–5	Youngest child is 6–12		
Weekdays						
Primary child caregiving	185	99	74	47	2.5	2.1
Total caregiving time	467	311	235	184	2.0	1.7
Weekends						
Primary child caregiving	132	58	90	40	1.5	1.4
Total caregiving time	557	456	454	398	1.2	1.1

Fathers' caregiving time, like that of mothers, differs by employment status, although employment status often means something very
different for men versus women. Nonemployment for fathers is a much
smaller category and is more likely to result from layoff or disability.
Nonetheless, using the four years' worth of the ATUS, we have sufficient sample sizes in all categories in order to consider the effect of
employment status on fathers as well as mothers. Figures 2.15a and
2.15b compare mothers and fathers by employment status for weekdays

Figure 2.15a Weekday Time Spent in Caregiving by Fathers and Mothers, by Employment Status

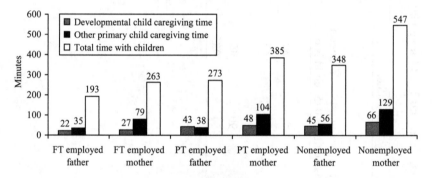

Figure 2.15b Weekend Time Spent in Caregiving by Fathers and Mothers, by Employment Status

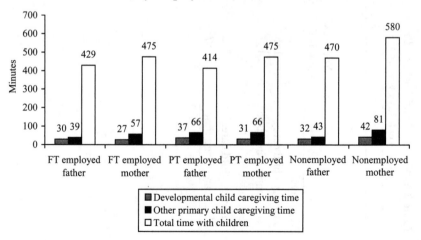

Table 2.7 Percent of Primary Child Caregiving Time That Is Developmental, by Employment Status and Weekdays versus Weekends for Mothers and Fathers

	Weekdays			Weekends		
	Mothers	Fathers	Significant difference	Mothers	Fathers	Significant difference
Full-time	23.0	33.8	***	27.1	35.5	***
Part-time	27.3	43.9	***	26.5	36.6	**
Not employed	30.2	42.2	***	27.8	42.9	***

NOTE: Asterisks represent results at t-tests of proportions between mothers and fathers. **significant at the 0.05 level; ***significant at the 0.01 level.

and weekends. Nonemployment by fathers on weekdays is associated with significantly more time in all three caregiving categories compared to full-time employed fathers. On weekends developmental caregiving time is essentially the same for full-time employed fathers and nonemployed fathers, but is approximately one-fourth higher for part-time employed fathers.

In these two figures, developmental caregiving and other primary caregiving are presented separately, as some authors have argued that fathers are more likely to do the "fun stuff" with children; that is, developmental care versus everyday physical care. Table 2.7 presents the proportion of fathers' developmental caregiving to all primary caregiving time, and clearly, this proportion is substantially higher for fathers than mothers, especially on weekdays. For full-time employed fathers on weekdays, 34 percent of their primary caregiving time is developmental compared to 23 percent for full-time employed mothers on weekdays and 28 percent for nonemployed mothers on weekdays. The consistently higher proportions for fathers do support the notion that fathers enjoy more "fun time" with children than do mothers.

THE TIME OF DAY PATTERN OF CAREGIVING TIME

Thus far, we have used the time diary information to sum up time spent in aggregated activity categories. In this section we use the timing of the activity to look at the pattern of caregiving time throughout the day. The rhythm of caregiving time is clear from the graphs presented in Figures 2.16 and 2.17. Especially on weekdays, primary caregiving is most likely to occur in the morning and in the evening. Of course, younger children receive more care, which is spread out more across the day, but there are still two noticeable peaks, in the morning and at night. Weekends dampen the peaks, especially for older children, who can be expected to get up and dress themselves on the weekend. But these same young school-aged children clearly need to be directed actively through their morning routines on weekdays.

Figures 2.18 and 2.19 look at the time of day of primary caregiving for the group of mothers with the greatest caregiving demands, those whose youngest child is aged 0–5. This set of figures compares the time of day of caregiving for 0–5-year-olds by two groups of mothers, those employed full time and those not employed. A much greater percent of nonemployed mothers are providing care at every hour of the day, especially on weekdays. On weekends, the percentages look more like the full-time employed mothers, but there are still more pronounced peaks in the morning and evening for full-time employed mothers on the weekend than nonemployed mothers. The most pronounced peaks are seen for full-time employed mothers on weekdays, where nearly a quarter of these mothers are engaged in caregiving activities at 8 a.m. and 9 p.m. and only 5 percent are engaged in caregiving activities at noon. In Chapter 5, we explore the covariance of the timing of employment and the timing of caregiving for those mothers who reported positive hours worked on their weekday diary days.

SUMMARY OF THE DESCRIPTIVE LOOK AT MOTHERS' CHILD CAREGIVING TIME

In this chapter, we provided an extensive overview of how mothers in the United States spend their time. We focused on five broad categories of time use: 1) paid work, 2) leisure, 3) primary caregiving, 4) home production, and 5) other. We find that for all mothers, primary caregiving falls on the weekends, but as expected, is greater for mothers of preschool-aged children than mothers of older children. Looking at alternative measures of caregiving, we find that reported minutes of

Figure 2.16 Percent of Mothers Whose Youngest Child is 0–5, Engaged in Primary Caregiving Activities, Weekdays and Weekends

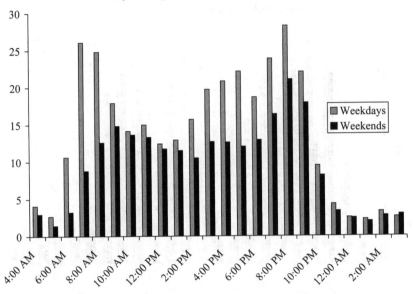

Figure 2.17 Percent of Mothers Whose Youngest Child is 6–12, Engaged in Primary Caregiving Activities, Weekdays and Weekends

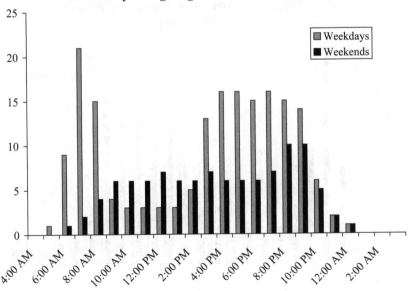

Figure 2.18   Percent of Full-Time Employed and Nonemployed Mothers Whose Youngest Child is 0–5, Engaged in Primary Caregiving Activities, Weekdays

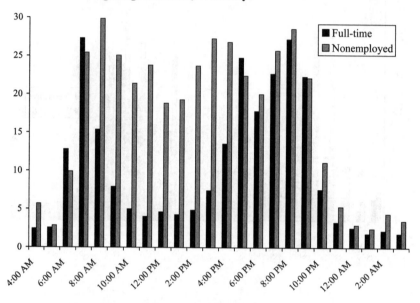

Figure 2.19   Percent of Full-Time Employed and Nonemployed Mothers Whose Youngest Child is 0–5, Engaged in Primary Caregiving Activities, Weekends

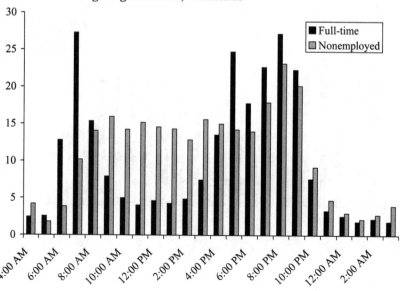

primary caregiving time vary more by the age of the mother's youngest child than the two alternative measures of secondary caregiving. Finally, we examined total caregiving time by summing primary caregiving and "time with children" and find that mothers of preschool-aged children devote nearly 8 hours to caregiving on weekdays and more than 9 hours on weekends compared to 6 hours and 7½ hours, respectively, for those whose youngest child is school-aged.

Moving beyond the caregiving focus, we examine the implication of caregiving responsibilities for time devoted to other activities. We find that the bulk of caregiving time is withdrawn from leisure and paid work, and this decline is greatest for mothers of preschool-aged children.

Next, we consider two important characteristics that we expect to be correlated with time use: marital status and employment. We find the married or cohabiting mothers spend more time caregiving on weekdays and weekends than unmarried mothers, regardless of the children's ages. The explanation seems to be related to employment hours. Unmarried women in our sample spend a greater percentage of their time on employment in every category. Additionally, we find that while employed mothers do devote less time to primary caregiving than their nonemployed counterparts, the reduction in caregiving time is approximately one hour a day, substantially less than the number of hours they are employed in the day.

We then turned to a comparison of mothers and nonmothers and finally to a comparison of mothers and fathers. We find that the biggest time difference between mothers and nonmothers is seen for full-time employed mothers who enjoy significantly less leisure than full-time employed nonmothers. Turning to mothers versus fathers, we find that mothers perform more caregiving than fathers, but the difference is smaller on the weekend. At the same time, we note that fathers enjoy over an hour more of leisure time on weekend days than mothers. Finally, digging deeper into subcategories of caregiving, we note that fathers' caregiving time is more likely to be "fun time" than mothers' caregiving time, who tend to focus their caregiving time on physical care for children.

In the final section of the chapter, we looked at the timing of caregiving and other activities across the diary day. We find that for most mothers, caregiving peaks in the morning hours and again in the evenings, but the timing across the day is smoother for nonemployed mothers.

Notes

1. The ATUS-defined 17 first-level time categories are Personal care; Household activities; Caring and helping household members; Caring and helping nonhousehold members; Work and work-related activities; Education; Consumer purchases; Professional and personal care services; Household services; Government service and civic obligations; Eating and drinking; Socializing, relaxing, and leisure activities; Sports, exercise, and recreation; Religious and spiritual activities; Volunteer activities; Telephone calls; and Travel.

2. This time categorization, motivated by economic theory, may not be familiar to time use researchers. Also, note that our "other" category is a combination of many different activities. Finally, note that we categorize travel time with the aggregate activity to which it was related. This is consistent with other time use researchers as described by Bittman and Wajcman (2004), who write, "The emerging standard is to assign traveling time to its associated purpose" (p. 172).

3. This bias may be relevant for our study if community connections affect access to child care.

4. In a future research project, we plan to use the German data to conduct a sensitivity analysis to determine the importance of using three days of data to construct a day average of time use versus using a single diary day of data.

5. In Chapter 3, we provide further evidence that reported primary caregiving is mainly structured time. In our multivariate analysis, we find that weekday caregiving time is significantly less in the summer, but weekend time does not differ by season. Finally, we have time of day evidence later in this chapter to show when the majority of child care is occurring. Caregiving is less bimodal on weekends than weekdays but the morning and evening "rushes" can still be seen on weekends, again arguing for reported caregiving time as being the routine structured time with children as opposed to just hanging out time on the weekend when everyone is around.

6. These percentages come from an analysis of the information of who else is in the room while the activity is taking place. In this case, we aggregated the leisure time when no one else was in the room and divided it by the total leisure time for each mother.

7. Not all primary caregiving time is time when one is responsible for a child, such as when a mother is making phone calls from work arranging a babysitter for the evening, but this type of arranging for care or transportation to facilitate care is only a small fraction of primary caregiving, so adding primary and secondary care together seems appropriate as a measure of total caregiving time.

8. Sleep, personal care time, and employment time are not probed for "with whom."

9. Because of the manner in which the questions were asked, it is possible that some of the time with children is not considered secondary child care time and vice versa. For example, if the children are upstairs playing while the mother is cooking dinner, she might report that she had children in her care while she was cooking but she was not with the children during that time. Alternatively, she might report

watching TV with her 12-year-old child but not think of that as time when that child was "in her care."

10. See Kalenkoski and Foster (2008) for further description of alternative measures of maternal caregiving.

11. Throughout this book, we include unmarried but cohabiting with the married group. Unmarried but cohabiting comprise 3 percent of the "married" sample. Kendig and Bianchi (2008) warn that those mothers who are unmarried but cohabiting are a heterogeneous group.

12. Note that Bianchi, Wight, and Raley (2005) find that maternal caregiving has declined for single mothers. This finding is supported by Sandberg and Hofferth (2001, 2005).

13. See Bianchi, Robinson, and Milkie (2006, Chapter 4) for further discussion of the relationship between maternal employment and maternal caregiving.

14. The time use of part-time employed mothers falls directly in between these two extremes.

15. Difference between nonemployed and part-time employed mothers of school-aged children is not significant, but difference between either and full-time employed mothers is significant.

16. Recall that the group of nonmothers includes mothers whose youngest child is a teenager.

3
The Nature of Maternal Caregiving

Is It More Like Leisure or Household Production?

The previous chapter provides a descriptive portrait of maternal time use in five aggregate uses categories: 1) home production, 2) caregiving, 3) leisure, 4) paid market work, and 5) other. In this chapter, we extend that analysis by relying on rigorous econometric techniques to estimate the effects of demographic and economic factors on time choices. Our focus on the first four time use categories (excluding other) expands the analysis beyond the traditional three categories of paid work, leisure, and home production. By explicitly separating caregiving from home production (the time use to which it typically is assigned), we are able to identify the factors specifically relevant to caregiving time choices. Additionally, our estimation strategy enables us to gain a better understanding of how mothers' caregiving time choices compare to their choices regarding other unpaid uses of time; specifically, household production and leisure time. If caregiving time responds differently in any substantive way to economic and demographic factors, then aggregating caregiving time into household production or leisure time in empirical research might yield mistaken empirical conclusions.

The main goal of the chapter is to describe the responsiveness of mothers' time use to economic factors. Toward this goal, we estimate market wage and child care price elasticities for each of four general categories of time use.[1] Other things equal, we find that all four time uses of mothers are responsive to their predicted wages, and caregiving time is sensitive to child care prices of preschoolers but not responsive to child care prices for school-aged children. Most interestingly, we find that higher-wage mothers devote more time to caregiving both on weekdays and weekends. Additionally, on weekdays, paid work time also responds positively to higher wages, while leisure time and home production time are reduced.[2] On weekends, only leisure and caregiving time are affected by higher wages, with leisure time decreased and caregiving increased for higher-wage mothers.

A second goal for this chapter is to better understand the importance of marital status, race, and other demographic factors in time choices, once economic factors have been controlled, and to determine whether these factors affect competing time choices differently. We showed in Chapter 2 that single mothers' caregiving and home production time were less than those of married or cohabiting women while their employment hours were greater.[3] We expect single mothers to make time use decisions differently from their married counterparts, in part due to the reduced possibility for specialization. With regard to race, previous research on the use of nonparental child care has revealed different child care utilization patterns by race, and we examine whether these differences carry over to maternal time use as well. Differences in time use by race may help explain racial differences in the gender wage gap or in wealth acquisition. Examining the role of race in time choices will allow us to identify the different roles that race could play in these very different activities.

MATERNAL TIME ALLOCATION

There is a long tradition among labor economists of relying on theoretical models that stratify all time use into two categories: paid work time and leisure (see, for example, Robbins [1930]). The New Home Economics models of the early 1960s acknowledge that a substantial portion of time not spent in paid employment is home production time, not leisure.[4] Since then, alternative approaches have focused on expanding the traditional two-dimensional time allocation model to three or more uses of time with the hope of disentangling activities that are unpaid yet behaviorally distinct from one another. Gronau (1977) and Graham and Green (1984) stratify time outside the labor market into home production and pure leisure. Gronau (1977) establishes two criteria for aggregating time uses and concludes that leisure time and home production time should not be combined. Gronau writes,

> From the theoretical point of view, the justification of aggregating leisure and work at home into one entity, nonmarket time (or home time) can rest on two assumptions: (a) the two elements react similarly to changes in the socioeconomic environment and therefore

nothing is gained by studying them separately, and (b) the two elements satisfy the condition of a composite input, that is, their relative price is constant and there is no interest in investigating the composition of the aggregate since it has no bearing on production and the price of the output. (p. 1100)

But in fact, Gronau's two criteria explain why, particularly for mothers, three uses of time are still not sufficient. In his model, unpaid "home work" is defined as time spent producing a good that could also be purchased in the market. In addition to home-produced goods and market-produced goods being indistinguishable, the home-production process in Gronau's model provides no enjoyment. However, home-produced child care (henceforth referred to as parental caregiving) is usually considered an imperfect substitute for market child care and certainly most parents receive pleasure from some of the portion of caregiving time (see, for example, Aguiar and Hurst [2007]). Thus, we believe it is best to avoid aggregating caregiving with either home production or leisure, and instead we expand the Gronau trinity into a model with four aggregated uses of time: 1) (paid) market work, 2) (unpaid) home work, 3) caregiving, and 4) leisure.[5]

The bulk of the previous literature that examines caregiving time focuses on couples, often dual earner households. Kooreman and Kapteyn (1987) look exclusively at married couples and find that higher wages of fathers increased the time their wives spent in caregiving, but that women's own wages affected neither's caregiving time. Nock and Kingston (1988) find that mothers' employment reduced their caregiving time, but that the reductions were mostly in secondary activities with children.[6] Using data from the Netherlands, for married mothers currently employed, Maassen van den Brink and Groot (1997) find no effect of husband's earnings on the time allocation of his wife in employment, home production, or caregiving. Closest to our research are the papers by Hallberg and Klevmarken (2003) and Kalenkoski, Ribar, and Stratton (2007). Hallberg and Klevmarken examine the determinants of parents' time allocated to caregiving in Sweden, and their structural model incorporates instruments for both parents' wages and parents' employment time. Their results differ substantially from ours in that they find that parents' own wages do not affect caregiving time of their sample of Swedish parents. Similarly, Kalenkoski, Ribar, and Stratton (2007), using British time diary data, find that mothers' wages have no effect on their own caregiving time on either week-days or weekends. However, earlier papers by Kalenkoski, Ribar, and Stratton (2005), using the same data without controlling for predicted wages, find that women with an advanced degree spend more time on primary caregiving, secondary caregiving, and market work. Similarly, Kalenkoski, Ribar, and Stratton (2007), using the ATUS, find that mothers with a bachelor's degree or a graduate degree spend more time on primary caregiving and in market employment.

Studies using more recent time diary data from the United States have found that employment hours negatively affect time spent with children; however, mothers appear to shield their children from the full impact of their employment by cutting back on personal time, sleep, leisure, and home production. Thus, there is some evidence that mothers treat caregiving time differently than either home production or leisure.[7] Sociologists have for some time made the distinction between child care and home production. Bianchi, Robinson, and Milkie (2006) show that, historically, housework time has declined while child care time has not. Sayer (2005) notes that over time, men and women have adjusted their nonmarket time substantially, concentrating mainly in their movement from unpaid home production into family time. Thus, the disaggregation of unpaid activities is becoming more important over time.[8]

DATA AND ESTIMATION STRATEGY

Data

Table 3.1 presents the average minutes spent in the four time categories, calculating means first including and then excluding those mothers with zero reported minutes in each activity. Looking at Table 3.1, we see substantial differences between weekdays and weekends in the time spent in the four activities. Leisure and home production times are higher on weekends while the opposite is true for employment and caregiving time. Using the means that exclude those mothers with zero reported minutes, the average number of weekday child care minutes equals 171 while the weekend mean is 142 minutes. The comparable minutes for household production are 223 minutes on weekdays and

Table 3.1 Average Minutes of Leisure, Caregiving, Home Production, and Employment

Dependent variables	Weekdays Mean (standard deviation) Sample size	Weekends Mean (standard deviation) Sample size
Means including zeros		
Minutes of caregiving	150.9	101.1
	(135.2)	(124.6)
	3,691	4,136
Minutes of employment	208.3	54.5
	(239.0)	(152.8)
	3,691	4,136
Minutes of home production	211.1	251.2
	(164.2)	(173.1)
	3,691	4,136
Minutes of leisure[a]	281.7	402.5
	(160.5)	(192.7)
	3,691	4,136
Means excluding zeros		
Minutes of caregiving	171.2	141.7
	(131.4)	(126.5)
	3,264	2,990
Minutes of employment	435.2	357.8
	(143.4)	(211.9)
	1,894	648
Minutes of home production	222.7	266.6
	(160.8)	(166.5)
	3,514	3,920

NOTE: Reported results are weighted to reflect population averages. Each cell contains the variable mean, standard deviation, and number of observations.
[a] There are very few mothers reporting zero minutes of leisure.
SOURCE: ATUS 2003–2006.

267 minutes on weekends. Regarding paid employment, the weekday mean is 435 while the weekend mean is 358, but note the dramatic drop in sample size for the weekend because the majority of mothers are not working for pay on those days. As already discussed in Chapter 2, less time is spent in caregiving on the weekend than weekdays, and substantially less time is spent in employment on the weekend. But as Figure 2.7 shows (p. 23), the reduction of primary caregiving time on the weekend is more than compensated by an increase in "time with children" and an increase in secondary child care. The differences in mean minutes of caregiving versus home production and leisure across days of the week provide suggestive evidence that time spent in child care is distinct from home production and leisure. Additionally, the dramatic differences in time use between weekdays and weekends serves to support our decision to estimate our time use models separately for those two diary day groups.

Further descriptive information is presented in Table 3.2, which shows the distribution of average time use by marital status and wage rate categories.[9] For example, looking at caregiving (and excluding those mothers with zero caregiving minutes), reported minutes for high-wage mothers vary significantly from 130 minutes for unmarried mothers to 203 minutes for married mothers. In addition, mothers differ significantly by wage level in the percent with nonzero reported caregiving minutes; 92 percent of high-wage unmarried mothers recording some minutes of caregiving on the diary day compared to 85 percent of married mothers. Interestingly, the married mothers devoting the most minutes to caregiving are in the high-wage category, which differs significantly from the mid-wage and low-wage categories, while the unmarried mothers devoting the most minutes to caregiving are in the low- and mid-wage category, which again differs significantly from the high-wage category. For married women, the result is consistent with Bryant and Zick's (1996) finding that more highly educated mothers spend more time in direct caregiving. Additionally, unmarried mothers at each wage level report similar minutes of paid work as married women, but differ by wage level on weekdays in the percent reporting zero minutes of employment on the diary day. On weekdays, married women are significantly more likely to report no employment minutes than unmarried mothers. On weekends, the percent of mothers with zero minutes of employment is high for both married and unmarried

Table 3.2 Average Minutes, by Marital Status and Wage Category, for Weekdays and Weekend Days

	Married			Unmarried		
	Low-wage	Mid-wage	High-wage	Low-wage	Mid-wage	High-wage
Weekday minutes spent in						
Paid work	439.2	432.9	426.6	439.9	441.8	446.7
	(71.4)	(49.3)	(49.2)	(60.7)	(40.8)	(26.4)
Caregiving	168.1	173.6	203.5	161.8	151.8	130.6
	(12.4)	(9.8)	(8.0)	(15.3)	(15.4)	(14.2)
Home production	274.9	232.8	225.1	201.6	179.8	196.5
	(1.7)	(4.3)	(3.9)	(7.0)	(6.1)	(8.5)
Leisure	308.5	276.8	266.8	330.8	278.9	269.4
	(0.4)	(0.3)	(0.2)	(0.9)	(0.7)	(0.0)
Weekend minutes spent in						
Paid work	430.7	347.2	216.6	422.3	416.2	265.7
	(88.8)	(86.0)	(82.9)	(81.7)	(81.5)	(81.9)
Caregiving	132.4	147.9	148.1	135.3	127.8	133.7
	(41.5)	(25.2)	(16.3)	(27.7)	(34.8)	(29.2)
Home production	285.2	273.6	280.7	214.8	246.9	282.5
	(7.0)	(4.1)	(3.5)	(10.4)	(6.5)	(4.2)
Leisure	384.3	404.5	415.8	400.3	406.4	413.0
	(0.0)	(0.1)	(0.0)	(0.0)	(0.6)	(0.0)

NOTE: Reported results are weighted to reflect population averages. The mid-wage category was calculated as the mean predicted wage plus or minus one standard deviation from the mean. Observations with zero reported minutes are excluded. Standard deviations are in parentheses.

SOURCE: ATUS 2003–2006.

mothers and is not statistically different between the groups. High-wage mothers, regardless of marital status, are significantly less likely to report any employment time on weekdays than low-wage mothers. On weekends, there is no significant difference in the percent reporting any employment time by wage level.

Estimation Strategy

The evidence presented in Table 3.2 is descriptive, but a fuller understanding of the relationship among time use, marital status, and wages requires a multivariate analysis. Our basic estimation model is a system of four time use equations shown in Equation 3.1.[10]

(3.1) $t_j = f(E, D, S)$,

where t_j is minutes of time in four aggregate categories of paid work, household production, caregiving, and leisure. These minutes of time are modeled as a function of E, a vector of economic factors; D, a vector of demographic factors; and S, a vector of time and spatial factors.

The key economic factors included in our analysis represent components of the price of time. These factors include the mother's hourly wage rate, the price of child care for preschool-aged children, and the price of child care for school-aged children. All three price of time measures were constructed with preliminary regressions that are explained in Appendix C.

Demographic factors relating to the individual mother include her age, education, and a pair of dichotomous variables indicating race and ethnicity: nonwhite (versus white), and Hispanic (versus non-Hispanic). These variables may reflect differences in time preferences or constraints. Studies of nonparental child care utilization have shown that nonwhites use more relative care than whites, so it is possible that nonwhite mothers will spend less time in caregiving (Capizzano, Tout, and Adams 2000; NCES 2004). Because hours of housework have declined substantially over time, we might expect an age cohort effect such that older women spend more time on home production than younger women (Bianchi 2000).

Demographic factors relating to the mother's family situation include the husband's earnings (if the mother is married), five measures of the number of children in the household for the following age categories: aged 0–2, 3–5, 6–9, 10–12, and 13–17, and two household status dichotomous variables for being married and having any other adults beyond oneself and one's spouse in the household. We expect that children of different ages contribute differently to the demands on mothers' time. Studies of the effect of the presence of children on mothers' employment have found differences between having a child aged 0–2 versus having a child aged 3–5. One reason for this difference is that many families view preschool as an educational investment in their children, not just as supervised time that facilitates women's employment; however, utilizing preschool does free up the mother's time while the children are at school. Children aged 6–9 are in school much of the day, but they are usually not left alone before and after school, while 10–12-year-olds are more often left alone.[11] The presence of other adults in the household may affect mothers' time use but the direction of the effect is not clear. A coresiding adult could contribute income to the household, thus allowing the mother to do more of the home production and caregiving, or this other adult could contribute child care and home production time, freeing up the mother for more employment time. The coresiding adult may also increase home production time, especially if this adult is an elderly relative who requires care.[12]

We do not have strong predictions from economic theory about the effect of marriage and husband's earnings on time use choices. The presence of the spouse should reduce child care and home production time to the extent that the husband participates in these tasks, but the demand for home production tasks also increases. We see in Table 3.2 that the presence of the spouse is significantly correlated with greater home production time for those women engaged in any home production and a lower probability of doing no home production on the diary day except among high-wage mothers. Assuming that her husband's employment time is exogeneous (still a reasonable assumption in our current labor market and standard in women's labor supply estimations), husband's earnings play the role of nonlabor income in our model.[13] Theoretically, higher levels of nonlabor income are expected to reduce all "work" time (employment and home production), and should increase leisure time, but the effect on caregiving depends on the weighting of the "work" versus the "consumption" components of caregiving time. However, higher nonlabor income may also mean a bigger house or more "stuff" to take care of, so even the effect on home production is ambiguous.

Variables included in the set of timing and spatial factors include a dichotomous variable that takes on the value of one if the diary was collected in June, July, or August and a value of zero otherwise. We expect that summer matters for mothers of young children due to school vacation and changes in the activities and even sleep patterns of children with the increased daylight hours and warmer temperatures. Additionally, we include two dichotomous location variables indicating residence in an urban area and residence in the south. These spatial regressors control for differences in the price of commodities and structural demands on one's time.

Recall that in Equation 3.1, we express the mother's time choice as a function of economic, demographic, and timing and spatial factors. The econometric methodology used to estimate this equation must accommodate the fact that the dependent variable (i.e., the minutes of time devoted to each of the four activities) may be zero in some cases.[14] As a result, the most common regression estimation strategy, Ordinary Least Squares, ought not be used for three of our four time uses.[15] Leisure is the only aggregate time category in which zero is almost never observed, thus OLS can be used for estimating the parameters of the determinants of leisure. For the other three time uses, we use a Tobit model, a nonlinear estimation technique that permits estimation of equations in which the dependent variable has a substantial number of zeros. We estimate these four equations jointly using a Seemingly Unrelated Regression model. This joint estimation helps account for the fact that all four time uses are observed on the same day.[16]

REGRESSION RESULTS

Empirical results are presented in Tables 3.3 (weekdays) and 3.4 (weekend). We conducted preliminary regressions to construct the wage and price measures as explained in Appendix C.[17] We estimate separate sets of regressions for weekdays and weekends since both theory and the descriptive analysis in Chapter 2 lead us to expect substantial differences between weekdays and weekend days. The institutional differences in the labor market and schools, as well as formal child care arrangements, suggest that caregiving choices will be different on weekdays and weekends. Connelly, DeGraff, and Willis (2004) find that child care arrangements differ substantially on Saturdays versus Monday through Friday. Mothers working on Saturday are more likely to use relatives, the child's father, or siblings as caregivers. Home-production time also is expected to differ on weekends and weekdays, as meal times may be less rigid on the weekends and larger blocks of time are available for housework projects. While it may not be the case that every demographic, economic, time, and spatial variable differs in its effect between weekend and weekdays, we expect that enough of them do to justify the separation of the sample between weekend and weekday.[18]

Results for Weekday Observations

Price of Time Variables

Similar to results from more standard household surveys like the CPS, the results in Table 3.3 show that employment minutes are increased and leisure is decreased when predicted wages are higher. Home production time is also decreased by an increase in wages, as would be predicted in the Gronau model, as women substitute time in the market for home production time. If caregiving time were like home production or leisure, we would expect that the wage effect of caregiving time would also be negative. However, that is not what we find. Instead, we find that an increase in the wage increases child caregiving time. In addition, this positive effect of an increase in mothers' hourly wage proves to be quite robust to changes in the sample and changes in the specification of the model.

What can explain the strong positive effect of wages on caregiving time for mothers? According to economic theory, wage changes include both an income effect and a substitution effect. The income effect leads to the prediction that when the wage increases thus increasing income, demand for most "goods" (including leisure) increases. The substitution effect, which is the result of the wage increase, causing the opportunity cost of one's time in unpaid activities to increase, leads to the prediction that less time will be devoted to all unpaid activities. As we discussed

Table 3.3 Weekday Marginal Effects of Determinants of Minutes Reported in Leisure, Caregiving, Home Production, and Employment

	Leisure	Caregiving	Home production	Employment
Predicted hourly log wage	-179.3923***	66.8999***	-83.8611***	223.8421***
Elasticities of hourly log	*-1.1896*	*0.3005*	*-0.4103*	*0.8066*
Predicted hourly price of child care for child aged 0–5	-1.1779	5.7670***	-0.7802	-2.6311
Elasticities of price of child care for child aged 0–5	*-0.0227*	*0.0753*	*-0.0111*	*-0.0275*
Predicted hourly price of child care for child aged 6–12	0.2902	-1.7949	-0.9297	2.3410
Elasticities of price of child care for child aged 6–12	*0.0039*	*-0.0165*	*-0.0093*	*0.0173*
Education	13.3872***	-5.7582**	1.8306*	-9.5063***
Age	1.9864***	0.2235	4.0454***	-4.4507***
Husband's monthly earnings, if married	5.0517***	4.7046***	6.6307***	-17.4628***
Married spouse present	-5.2146	-19.1993***	25.5751***	22.8488**
Nonwhite	-1.8392	-19.8202***	-12.7279**	1.2029
Hispanic	-33.9721***	-13.1694**	13.0796	10.7788
No. of children aged 0–2	-21.8122***	80.9271***	34.2717***	-84.7334***
No. of children aged 3–5	-4.7149	28.3806***	26.0214***	-38.7390***
No. of children aged 6–9	2.4205	24.8636***	21.4091***	-33.5462***
No. of children aged 10–12	1.6403	8.1693**	21.4036***	-18.6586**
No. of children aged 13–17	-3.7874	-1.8405	13.4984***	-4.6195

Presence of other adult in household	−3.0289	−8.3155	10.2771	−15.4011
Urban	21.7718***	5.4253	9.8491**	−53.2525***
South	−12.4224**	12.0411***	−18.7355***	16.6397**
Summer	18.6433***	−31.0932***	5.8001	2.8150

NOTE: Husband's monthly earnings are in thousands of dollars; predicted prices of child care and hourly log wages are derived from preliminary regression analyses. Predicted hourly price of child care is set to zero for mothers with no children in that age category.
*significant at the 0.10 level; **significant at the 0.05 level; ***significant at the 0.01 level.
SOURCE: ATUS 2003–2006.

Table 3.4 Marginal Effects of Determinants of Minutes Spent in Leisure, Caregiving, Home Production, and Employment—Weekends

	Leisure	Child care	Home production	Employment
Predicted hourly log wage	−80.0529*	157.1215***	−19.0775	12.8997
Elasticities of hourly log	*−0.8046*	*2.9424*	*−0.0744*	*0.0317*
Predicted hourly price of child care for child aged 0–5	−4.6184*	4.5340***	4.1353*	10.4239
Elasticities of price of child care for child aged 0–5	*−0.1387*	*0.2538*	*0.0482*	*0.0766*
Predicted hourly price of child care for child aged 6–12	3.7042	−9.1098***	4.0943*	−1.2778
Elasticities of price of child care for child aged 6–12	*0.0752*	*−0.3446*	*0.0323*	*−0.0063*
Education	9.9141**	−9.9236**	−0.3912	6.3994
Age	0.4602	−1.0997	3.5339***	−1.4471
Husband's monthly earnings, if married	2.3437	2.9388**	−1.1059	−11.0239**
Married spouse present	−0.6155	−9.4991	19.9892**	−12.6420
Nonwhite	12.8232	−17.2042***	−30.6173***	−37.6959
Hispanic	−9.1712	−18.6766***	6.3003	−20.1696
No. of children aged 0–2	−15.2089	83.1075***	−6.0967	−103.5704***
No. of children aged 3–5	−1.5378	21.4092***	1.1391	−48.5263
No. of children aged 6–9	−5.2140	19.3523***	5.6862	−15.3307
No. of children aged 10–12	−11.7075**	−10.2938**	20.4878***	−2.2686
No. of children aged 13–17	−4.2860	−8.7078*	12.2576**	19.1951

Presence of other adult in household	−18.3325**	16.1246**	−20.8080**	54.4345**
Urban	15.8752*	−12.4081*	−1.8468	−4.9925
South	5.8957	5.1016	−1.0131	−15.4335
Summer	10.8100	−12.2298**	3.7346	14.1619

NOTE: Husband's monthly earnings are in thousands of dollars; predicted prices of child care and hourly log wages are derived from preliminary regression analyses. Predicted hourly price of child care is set to zero for mothers with no children in that age category. *significant at the 0.10 level; **significant at the 0.05 level; ***significant at the 0.01 level.
SOURCE: ATUS 2003–2006.

above, for women, the substitution effect usually outweighs the income effect for leisure and home production, because women's wages and work hours are lower than men's and women spend a greater percent of their time in home production activities. But the caregiving results in Table 3.3 imply that for caregiving, the income effect outweighs the substitution effect. One can speculate about why the income effect for caregiving time is so strong. We believe that one of the mechanisms at work is that higher income (via higher wages) increases the demand for high-quality caregiving, and that high-quality caregiving requires more maternal time. In addition, in response to an increase in the wage, mothers can substitute time away from home production and away from leisure toward more caregiving time without having to reduce employment time. Third, caregiving time has a large investment component. Parents of young children invest time and money in high-quality caregiving in order to reap a future benefit of more emotionally healthy, more attached children, with higher levels of human capital. These "higher-quality children" on average will do better in school, and in the labor market, and will be more likely to stay emotionally involved with their parents. The production function of high-quality children takes substantial amounts of maternal time—time that cannot be purchased in the marketplace.

Our findings contradict those of Hallberg and Klevmarken (2003); Kalenkoski, Ribar, and Stratton (2007); and Kooreman and Kapteyn (1987), who all find that own wages do not affect caregiving time. Those studies, however, were undertaken using data from very different cultural settings and time periods. One difference between Kalenkoski, Ribar, and Stratton (2007) and our model is that their study includes mothers of children under age 18 while we limit our analysis to mothers of preteens. The caregiving time of mothers of older children may be more independent of their wages.

Other researchers have noted the positive relationship between higher income and caregiving time. Hill and Stafford (1974) find that high-wage mothers spend more time on caregiving and hypothesize that the purpose is to invest more heavily in their children. Ramey and Ramey (2008) argue that highly educated parents invest more time in their children in order to prepare their children better for the competition of college admissions in the United States.

A higher price for child care for children aged 0–5 makes nonparental child care more expensive and thus reduces the demand for nonparental child care and increases the amount of maternal caregiving time. Since very young children need to be cared for by someone, a decline in the amount of nonparental child care must be accompanied by an increase in maternal caregiving time. The price of child care for children 0–5 is only applied to those women with children in that age range; thus, the marginal effect is the effect of having a very young child and the estimated hourly cost of that care. The price of child care for older children did not have a significant effect on mothers' time choices. This suggests that there exists more flexibility in choices of child care options for school-aged children, including the possibility of self-care.

To interpret the size of economic variables' marginal effects, we can use the elasticities that are presented in Table 3.3.[19] For weekday diaries, three of the elasticities are less than 1 in absolute value, implying that for employment, caregiving, and home production, mothers are relatively insensitive to the price of time as it is affected by wages and the price of nonparental child care. A 10 percent increase in the wage leads to an 8 percent increase in time spent in weekday employment, a 4 percent decline in weekday home production time, and a 3 percent increase in time spent in weekday caregiving.[20] Leisure is the most elastic use of time; it declines by 12 percent for a 10 percent increase in wages. The elasticities of caregiving time with respect to both child care prices are much smaller in absolute value than the wage elasticities. A 10 percent increase in the price of caregiving for preschoolers increases caregiving time by 0.75 percent.

Demographic variables

As we have already observed with the wage effects, a quick glance across the rows of demographic variables in Table 3.3 confirms the descriptive findings of Table 3.2 that caregiving is distinct from both leisure and home production. For example, the effect of maternal age on time use (recall we are controlling for wage levels and number of children) is to increase home production and leisure, and decrease employment time, but it has no effect on caregiving time or leisure. Being married increases home production time and paid work time but decreases caregiving time and has no effect on leisure. Having controlled for marital status, increased husband's earnings, which can be thought of as nonlabor income from the mother's perspective, was expected to decrease all "work" activities. However, home production time and child care time on weekdays are both significantly positively related to husband's earnings while employment time is negatively related. These results are consistent with the hypothesis that higher-income families demand higher levels (either quality or quantity) of caregiving as well as home production activities, and these higher levels require more time inputs. Alternatively, mothers whose husbands have higher earnings may do a greater share of the caregiving and home production.

Race and ethnicity have some significant effects on mothers' time use. Nonwhites spend 20 fewer minutes on caregiving time and 13 fewer minutes on home production than whites, everything else held constant. This may be related to their increased use of relatives as caregivers (Capizzano, Tout, and Adams 2000; NCES 2004). Hispanic mothers have 34 fewer minutes of leisure time.

As we would expect, having very young children (aged 0–2) increases women's time in child care on weekdays substantially. Each additional child in that age range results in 81 extra minutes of child care time. That extra time per infant comes mainly from reduced employment time (85 minutes), but leisure time is also reduced by 22 minutes, while home production time is increased by 34 minutes. Older children (aged 3–5, 6–9, and 10–12) have very similar effects on women's time, but the effects are substantially smaller in magnitude except for home production time, which is constant across children's age groups. For older children, leisure time is no longer reduced significantly. Teenagers seem to have no effect on mothers' time during the week except for home production time, which is increased by 13 minutes on weekdays.

Finally, the last household characteristic included is the presence of other adults in the household. The presence of these adults does not affect any of the four uses of time. This result contrasts with Kalenkoski, Ribar, and Stratton (2007), who find negative effects of other adults present on mothers' weekday caregiving, both primary and passive. However, in our model, the presence of other adults is allowed to affect the probability of using paid child care, which affects the price of child care. The price of child care for children 0–5 is shown in Table 3.3 to affect time use choices, as discussed above.

Timing and Spatial Characteristics

On weekdays, mothers living in urban areas have fewer employment hours and more leisure and household production time than mothers living in rural areas, while mothers in the southern part of the United States have less leisure and household production time than those in the rest of the country. The season in which the diary was collected affects time use, with summer weekdays being a time of less child care (31 minutes) and more leisure time (18 minutes) than weekdays during the rest of the year. It is interesting that summer should affect child care time in this way since during the summer, school is not providing the care that it does during the school year for school-aged children. It appears that the self-reported primary child caregiving time is more rigidly tied to regular weekday routines, and that summer loosens our routines, reducing the time that is categorized as caregiving time. Kalenkoski, Ribar, and Stratton (2007), using the same data, also find that summer substantially reduces women's weekday primary caregiving time. They find that women's weekday passive caregiving time increases in the summer by about as many minutes as primary caregiving time is reduced.

To explore a bit further the differences between time use in the summer and the rest of the year, Table 3.5 presents the percent of time allocated to the five categories by weekday versus weekend and the age of the youngest child. The asterisks represent significance levels for simple t-tests of the means. Table 3.5 shows that mothers whose youngest child is 6–12 experience the largest percentage changes in caregiving time on weekdays across the seasons. The time lost from caregiving in the summer appears as increased leisure. Paid work, home production, and other are unaffected by the time of year from which the time use data are drawn.

Table 3.6 disaggregates primary child care time into developmental and nondevelopmental time using the same definitions we used in Chapter 2. Again, it is mothers whose youngest child is school-aged who experience the largest differences in caregiving between summer and the rest of the year, particularly on weekdays. The percent of primary caregiving time that is developmental falls from 37 percent the rest of the year to 18 percent during the summer months.

Table 3.5 Percent of Mothers' Time, by Age of Youngest Child, Summer/Not Summer, and Weekday/Weekend

	Weekdays				Weekends			
	Youngest child is 0–5		Youngest child is 6–12		Youngest child is 0–5		Youngest child is 6–12	
	Not summer	Summer	Not summer	Summer	Not summer	Summer	Not summer	Summer
Caregiving	13.3	12.1***	7.6	5.0***	9.4	8.6*	4.3	3.5***
Leisure	18.3	19.5**	19.5	21.6***	26.7	28.3***	28.7	30.5**
Paid work	13.1	13.2	18.7	18.1	3.7	3.5	4.1	4.9
Home production	14.3	14.8	14.3	14.8	16.9	16.9	18.9	17.9*
Other	41.0	40.4	40.0	40.5	43.4	42.7	43.9	43.3

NOTE: Sample weights used. Asterisks represent results of t-test of proportions across seasons. *significant at the 0.10 level; **significant at the 0.05 level; ***significant at the 0.01 level.
SOURCE: ATUS 2003–2006.

Table 3.6 Minutes of Caregiving Time, by Age of Youngest Child, Summer/Not Summer, and Weekday/Weekend

	Weekdays				Weekends			
	Youngest child is 0–5		Youngest child is 6–12		Youngest child is 0–5		Youngest child is 6–12	
	Not summer	Summer	Not summer	Summer	Not summer	Summer	Not summer	Summer
Developmental caregiving	56	57	37	18***	45	40	21	16**
Nondevelopmental caregiving	135	117***	72	54***	90	84	42	34***
Time with children excluding primary caregiving time	274	294**	187	264***	420	441**	398	408
Total time with children	465	468	296	336***	555	565	460	458
% of primary caregiving time that is developmental	29.5	32.6*	34.0	24.8***	33.5	32.1*	33.4	31.2**

NOTE: Sample weights used. Asterisks represent results of t-test of proportions across seasons. *significant at the 0.10 level; **significant at the 0.05 level; ***significant at the 0.01 level.
SOURCE: ATUS 2003–2006.

Results for Weekend Observations

Price of Time Variables

Recall that on weekdays, a higher hourly wage decreased leisure and home production time while increasing caregiving and employment. On weekends, a higher hourly wage continues to impact leisure and caregiving time as it did on weekdays, but home production time and employment time are unaffected by wages. Why do mothers with higher wages do less housework on weekdays but appear no different statistically from other mothers on the weekend? Partly, we may be observing the shifting of time from weekdays to weekends. Some home production tasks, such as laundry, housecleaning, and grocery shopping, are fungible throughout the week, while others such as meal preparation are less fungible. These results seem to support the hypothesis posited by Hamermesh and Lee (2007), namely that high-income women face a significant time crunch because of the high value of their time; they experience less leisure and more caregiving time than low-wage women every day of the week, with more employment hours on weekdays and home production hours simply deferred to weekends.

The price of child care for children 0–5 is a significant positive predictor of minutes spent in caregiving on the weekend, but the effect is smaller in magnitude than it was for weekdays. Paradoxically, a higher price of child care for children 6–12 is associated with fewer hours of child care on the weekend. This may be related to a greater use of teenagers, other adults, and husbands (if married) for weekend caregiving than for weekday caregiving.

Table 3.4 also records the elasticities of time use with respect to the price of time measure. The magnitudes of the elasticities are smaller on weekends versus weekdays except for the effect of the hourly wage on child care time, which shows substantially more elasticity on the weekend. Specifically, a 10 percent increase in the wage causes a 3 percent increase in caregiving on weekdays but a 29 percent increase in caregiving on weekends. Thus, higher-wage women spend more time in caregiving on weekdays and substantially more time in caregiving on weekends compared to lower-wage women. This positive investment of time may be expected to translate into higher levels of school readiness and school achievement for the children of higher-wage mothers, although outcome-based research is needed to confirm the connection between increased maternal caregiving time and these child outcomes.

Demographic variables

Considering the regression results for weekends, we concentrate our discussion on differences between weekdays and weekends. While most of the demographic variables follow very similar patterns on both weekends and weekdays, there are fewer significant differences. The effect of husband's earnings is smaller for weekends than weekdays, and married mothers differ from unmarried mothers on the weekends only in household production, with married mothers performing 20 more minutes of household production than unmarried mothers on weekends.[21] Also, Southern mothers do not differ from non-Southern mothers in their weekend time use.

Focusing on demographic variables relating to household composition reveals interesting weekend differences in time use. The presence of an infant does not decrease women's leisure on the weekend, nor does it affect household production. Instead, the increased caregiving time on weekends related to having an infant results from substantially reduced employment time compared to mothers with older children. The effect of older children in the household is also interesting. While older children do not affect leisure on weekdays (perhaps because there is not much leisure on weekdays for mothers), the presence of children aged 10–12 does reduce weekend leisure. Older children increase caregiving time and household production on weekends much as they do on weekdays, except on weekends, children aged 10–12 reduce caregiving time.

Another interesting difference between weekends and weekdays is the effect of other adults on mothers' time use, which, recall, has no influence on mothers' time choices on weekdays. On weekends, having another adult in the household (other than a husband) does have a substantial effect on mothers' time choices. Mothers with another adult in the household are employed 54 more minutes, perform 16 more minutes of caregiving, devote 21 fewer minutes to household production, and have 18 fewer minutes of leisure on a weekend.

Timing and Spatial Characteristics

During the summer, mothers spend 30 fewer minutes caregiving on weekdays and 12 fewer minutes caregiving on weekends; summer has no impact on other time uses. The smaller effect of summer on weekend versus weekday caregiving provides further evidence that activities self-reported as caregiving are the more structured interactions with children. Weekends, like summer, appear to be less structured, so that weekends in the summer are more similar to weekends in the rest of the year than the comparison of weekdays across seasons. It may be the structured nature of primary child care time that causes it to respond in many ways more similar to work than to either home production or leisure.

Correlation between Time Uses on Weekdays and Weekends

The Seemingly Unrelated Regression strategy takes into account correlations among the error terms of the four time use equations. Table 3.7 shows the pairwise trade-off between time uses on both weekdays and weekends. Most of the correlations are negative, indicating time trade-offs. The one exception is weekday child care time and home production time, which has a small positive relationship. As child caregiving time increases on weekdays so does home production. This could be because both activities happen at home and both have supervisory aspects that can allow mothers to alternate between activities. However, the negative relationship between these two time uses does exist on the weekend. The negative trade-offs between employment time and home production time and between leisure and employment are much larger than the trade-off of employment and child care and leisure and child care. This is still further evidence that child care time is behaving like neither home production nor leisure.

SUMMARY

Our extension of the Gronau (1977) model is based on the idea that caregiving activities may be composed of a unique set of activities

Table 3.7 Cross-Equation Correlations for Both Weekdays and Weekends

	Leisure	Caregiving	Home production	Employment
Weekdays				
Leisure	1			
Child care	−0.1793***	1		
Home production	−0.0305	0.0393**	1	
Employment	−0.4675***	−0.2761***	−0.6123***	1
Weekends				
Leisure	1			
Caregiving	−0.2659***	1		
Home production	−0.4525***	−0.0831***	1	
Employment	−0.4074***	−0.0847***	−0.2557***	1

NOTE: **significant at the 0.05 level; ***significant at the 0.01 level.
SOURCE: ATUS 2003–2006.

that are not appropriately aggregated with either home production or leisure. The empirical results presented here provide strong support for this hypothesis, suggesting that aggregating caregiving with leisure or with home production would be inappropriate for reasons first outlined by Gronau. Caregiving time does not behave like either leisure or home production in its response to the predicted prices of time, demographic differences, or timing and spatial differences. In addition, child care does not simply take the middle road between leisure and home production. Instead, child care time behaves quite distinctly from both of these time uses. Indeed, higher maternal wages decreased both leisure time and home production (on weekdays), as standard home production theory would predict, while caregiving time (like employment time) was increased.

The determinants of caregiving time were mostly as predicted. We expected that more children and younger children would result in more caregiving time, and we found strong evidence of this. The evidence also suggests that married or partnered women spend less time on weekday child care, as their partners are also available for care. Higher-earning husbands reduce the mother's hours of employment, and some of that increased time is devoted to caregiving. Increasing the price of market child care for preschoolers also has the expected effect of increasing maternal caregiving time, as some mothers substitute away from market child care for maternal caregiving, especially on weekdays. All of these findings give us faith both in these new data and our estimation procedure.

The one notable empirical result is that higher wages are associated with more caregiving time. However, this finding should not surprise us. Child care and employment both share a strong investment component. One reason salaried employees often work more hours than hourly employees is to invest in their future wage growth. Caregiving time often is devoted to the production of child quality, the benefits of which will not be reaped for many years to come. In addition, structured child care time may be less fungible within the week than home production, especially for very young children. Children need to be put to bed every night and homework needs to be supervised most weeknights, while the laundry and the dirty kitchen floor can wait until the weekend. Thus, we can understand the pattern that emerges from the descriptive comparison of weekdays and weekends, as shown in Table 3.1—that child care time is lower on the weekends than weekdays, but home production and leisure are greater on the weekends.

In part, our findings of the positive wage effect on caregiving may be driven by our choice to define caregiving time as primary child caregiving activities, thereby excluding activities in which children are present but caregiving is not reported as the primary activity.[22] Several other researchers have found that mothers have shielded children from the bulk of their increase in paid employment by reducing their leisure and housework time (Bianchi 2000; Howie et al. 2006; Sandberg and Hofferth 2001; Sayer, Bianchi, and Robinson 2004). If we had included those minutes of leisure or home production where mothers are also engaged in supervisory child care as caregiving time, we might have dissipated the positive wage effect on primary child care. But if mothers are even minimally accurate in categorizing the time when children are the primary focus of their attention as caregiving time, then we must expect that the investment aspect of this primary caregiving time is greater, and that the result we have observed has real-life consequences for child outcomes that are affected by the amount of caregiving time the children receive from their mothers.

Concerning the demographic determinants of child care time, married and partnered women differ significantly from single mothers in their weekday time use. On weekends, however, being married is not a significant predictor of any of the time uses except home production. Married women with higher-earning husbands spend less time in employment and more time on caregiving, home production, and leisure on weekdays. Only caregiving time is increased with higher-income husbands on the weekends, while paid work time is reduced.

One of the contributions this chapter makes to the literature on mothers' time use is the estimation of time use models that include wages and the price of child care, thereby facilitating direct discussion of policy implications. Predicted wages and the price of child care each have significant effects on time use decisions. Given our findings, including the strong correlations found between time uses, any policy that alters the opportunity cost of engaging in unpaid activities will have repercussions for all uses of time. Those policies would include tax policy, the Earned Income Tax Credit, and welfare policy, as each affects the net value of time in the labor market. Health care policy that affects who lives with whom and also the value beyond wages of being employed can also be expected to affect mothers' time use. Finally, policymakers thinking about school readiness should be interested in our finding that high-wage mothers spend more time on caregiving, as well as being able to afford higher quality nonparental care. Overcoming that double inequality of both time and money investments may mean that our national child care policy should be more focused on low-income families.

We have presented a substantial number of results given the four uses of time, the necessary distinction between weekdays and weekends, and the large number of demographic, household, and price of time variables. What big picture lessons can we take away from this analysis? First, the time diary results, despite recall error and a single day of observation, are in line with the basic predictions from more traditional household surveys, such as a positive relationship between wages and employment time, a negative relationship between wages and leisure time, and the prediction that more children increases the caregiving and home production time of the mother. Second, and perhaps most important, we believe we have provided convincing evidence of the importance of treating caregiving as a distinct time usage. Third, our results show that researchers must think carefully about the movement of time across days of the week and across seasons. Some tasks must be done at a specific time each day, while others are fungible across the week and even across the year. Finally, our findings suggest that high-wage mothers are particularly time pressed. They spend more time on child care and employment during the week with less time for leisure and home production. On the weekend, they spend equal time in home production as lower-wage mothers, as well as more time on child care and less in leisure. This is suggestive evidence of a time crunch (whether self-chosen or not) that requires further investigation.[23]

Notes

1. The term "elasticities" is explained later in this chapter.
2. Note that this is employment time on a given day, not total employment time.
3. In this chapter, as in Chapter 2, we combine married and cohabiting mothers into a category we call married.
4. See, most importantly for our purpose here, Becker (1965), Graham and Green (1984), and Gronau (1977).
5. The remaining activities are collapsed into a fifth category that includes sleep, personal care time, education, and job seeking endeavors, and can be thought of loosely as personal investment time. Maassen van den Brink and Groot (1997) use four categories of time use: leisure, home production, child care, and employment. Kooreman and Kapteyn's (1987) model includes eight categories.
6. Both papers use data from U.S time diaries from the 1975–1981 Time Use Longitudinal Panel.
7. For examples of this research, see Howie et al. (2006), Bianchi, Wight, and Raley (2005), Reimer (2002), Sandberg and Hofferth (2001), Bianchi (2000), and Bryant and Zick (1996).
8. Sayer (2005) and Craig (2006) both note that while men are adjusting their unpaid time in response to mothers' increased paid work time, the result thus far is not one of gender equity in all time uses. One positive outcome of the time use evolution (as noted by Sayer, Bianchi, and Robinson [2004]) is that parental time investments in their children have increased, contrary to much media reporting.
9. The middle-wage category is defined as the approximate mean wage in the full sample ($10) plus and minus one standard deviation ($2.00), and thus includes wages in the $8–$12 per hour range. Thus, a low wage is a wage less than $8 an hour and a high wage is a wage greater than $12 an hour. Note also that the wage measure used here is the predicted wage measure generated from preliminary estimation. This predicted wage is created using a standard two-step Heckman (1979) correction. For details, see Appendix C.
10. Our estimation model is derived from an underlying utility maximization model as described in Kimmel and Connelly (2007). Broadly speaking, the behavioral model underlying our empirical specification is the standard individual-based util-

ity maximizing problem in which a mother's utility is expressed as a function of leisure, child services, and aggregated adult consumption of final goods and services excluding child services. On the constraint side of the model, there is a mother's time constraint, the child's total caregiving time constraint, and a budget constraint. These three constraints imply that the wage and child care prices must enter the estimating equations separately.

11. Using the SIPP data from Winter 2002, Overturf Johnson (2005) reports that 7 percent of elementary school children are in self-care compared with 33 percent of middle school children (pp. 12–13). Casper and Smith (2004) use the 1995 SIPP data and report that 6.8 percent of 5–7-year-olds were in self-care compared with 16.0 percent of 8–10-year-olds and 25.2 percent of 11–13-year-olds. There does not seem to be any consensus about age groupings in this literature. In our estimation, we were looking for as much detail as possible without making our models unwieldy.

12. We have included care of other household members in the home production category.

13. Mroz (1987) tested this and many other assumptions of the standard labor supply model and found that the assumption of husband's earnings exogeneity was not rejected. More recently, Blau and Kahn (2007) find that if anything, husband's employment has less of an effect on women's labor supply in 2000 than it did it 1980. Note that Blau and Kahn also assume exogeneity of husband's earnings. See Chapter 4 for a fuller treatment of the effect of one's husband's choices on married mothers' choices.

14. Recall that Table 3.1 reveals substantial differences in means for samples including zeroes versus samples excluding zeroes.

15. There is some disagreement among time use researchers about whether Tobits or OLS are more appropriate for this type of estimation. The discussion centers on whether the zeroes observed are true zeroes or simply zero on the diary day. Tobit is seen as a better choice if the values are true zeroes.

16. See Kimmel and Connelly (2007) for further detail.

17. See regressor descriptive statistics in Appendix C, Table C.1 (p. 142). Note that these tables present marginal effects evaluated at the sample means. For the three economic variables, elasticities are also presented at the sample means. The models are estimated without sample weights, but this should not affect the interpretation of the multivariate analysis since determinants of nonrandom sampling, particularly the oversampling of weekends, is modeled in the specification.

18. Since this expectation rests on institutional differences between days of the week, it is different from analyzing days with employment time versus days without employment time. First, not all the mothers in our sample are employed, and even if they are employed on weekends, other differences in who else is available and what other activities they are engaged in are expected to differ between weekends and weekdays. We tested the four time use equations separately, fully interacting the other independent variables and weekend status. In the leisure equation, only the Hispanic variable differed between weekends and weekdays, but for caregiving time, the number of children aged 0–2, 3–5, 6–9, and 10–12; the presence of

another adult; and summer all differed significantly at the 5 percent level between weekdays and weekends. For employment, husband's earnings, marital status, number of children 6–9, and presence of another adult all differed between weekdays and weekends. Finally, for home production, husband's earnings; the number of children aged 0–2 and 6–9; and the presence of other adults differed between weekdays and weekends. The pattern of variables that differ between weekdays and weekends supports our contention that it is the institutional time of work, formal child care, and school that makes weekends and weekdays different since it is the presence of children and other adults that leads to differences between weekday and weekend time choices.

19. A price elasticity measures the percentage change in minutes arising from a 1 percent change in the price. For example, a wage elasticity equal to −0.1 implies that a 10 percent increase in the wage leads to a 1 percent reduction in time devoted to that activity.

20. This estimate of the wage elasticity of paid work hours is within the range of results found by other researchers. See, for example, Mroz (1987) and Kaufman and Hotchkiss (2003).

21. It is possible that permitting all coefficients to vary by marital status would produce different results. We hope to pursue this extension in future research.

22. Our findings are not driven by the choice to exclude sleep and personal care time from leisure or by the choice to concentrate on mothers of children under age 13 instead of age 18. We performed both of these alternative analyses, and the main results are robust to these changes.

23. See Hamermesh and Lee (2007) for a cross-national comparison of time crunch.

4

Husbands' Influences on
Mothers' Unpaid Time Choices

Among the key results from the previous chapter are the importance of marital status and spousal income on mothers' time use. Being married or cohabiting increases home production time on both weekdays and weekends and increases employment and reduced caregiving time on weekdays. Higher spousal income is associated with more leisure time, less employment time, more caregiving time, and more home production on weekdays. The effect of husbands' higher earnings on weekends is more muted but still increases mothers' caregiving time and lowers their employment time. In this chapter, we pursue further the role of marital status with an added focus on how husbands' weekly employment hours and husbands' time in an unpaid activity affect mothers' time in the same unpaid activity. We also consider the role of relative wages, that is, a mother's wage relative to her husband's in affecting time choices of mothers. Blau and Kahn (2007) show that wives' labor supply decisions are affected less by spousal factors than they once were, but no such evidence exists concerning unpaid uses of time. Thus, in this chapter we examine three types of out-of-market time: leisure, home production, and caregiving time.

PREVIOUS RESEARCH ON MARRIED COUPLES' JOINT TIME USE DECISION MAKING

In order to think about the role that husbands' time choices may play in mothers' time decision making, consider the underlying reasons for marriage that can be gleaned from economic models. These models of marriage emphasize the "gains from marriage," namely, the improvement in well-being upon marriage, which serves to motivate each potential partner to form a partnership. This gain can come from gains from specialization or gains from complementarities. Gains from specialization rely on the existence of fairly fixed quantities of requisite household goods that can be produced by either the husband or the wife. For example, if dinner needs to be cooked, one member of the couple may do the cooking while the other tends to the children or even reads the newspaper. Thus, we might expect that increased home production time of the husband would reduce the home production time of the wife.

If the gains from marriage arise from complementarities, such as enjoying spending leisure time with one's spouse, then we would predict that an increase in the leisure time of one spouse would increase the leisure time of the other spouse. Hamermesh (2002), Hallberg (2003), and Jenkins and Osberg (2005) find evidence of this desire for simultaneous leisure. Having tastes similar to one's spouse also increases the gains from marriage (Lam 1988) and may lead to positive correlations in time use other than leisure. For example, if a man who values living in a neat house marries a woman who also values living in a neat house, then they likely both spend more time on home production.[1]

The household bargaining model literature provides another theoretical framework for understanding why a husband and wife's time use might be related. Bargaining model proponents extend the unitary model of household decision making proposed by Becker (1991) by arguing that the source of income within a family is an important determinant of who ultimately consumes the items "purchased" by the family, including leisure. The relative wage is expected to determine power within the household for a variety of reasons.[2]

Unpaid housework has been a particular research focus in the area of couples' time allocation, in part because changes in women's labor supply have not brought equal changes in the distribution of unpaid tasks within the household. While women have substantially reduced their home production time and men have somewhat increased theirs, women continue to do a majority of the family's housework (Fisher et al. 2006). Evidence shows that women perform more unpaid home production than their male counterparts, while marital status is positively related with household production time for women but not men.[3]

For additional evidence on the role of spouses in time use choices in the United States, we turn to previous research based, like ours, on time diary studies. Kooreman and Kapteyn (1987) use U.S. time diary data from 1975–1976 for dual earner couples and find that the husband's own wages and his wife's wages have little effect on seven different types of nonmarket time. Solberg and Wong (1992) use U.S. data from 1977–1978 to estimate time use for husbands and wives in three aggregate categories: leisure, household production, and paid work. They find that the husband's household production is unaffected by either his wage or his wife's wage.[4] An example of research using more recent data is Kalenkoski, Ribar, and Stratton (2009), who use data from the United Kingdom to examine the role of wages on parents' time choices in three activities: primary caregiving, secondary caregiving, and paid work time. They find that spousal wages are, for the most part, unimportant in parental time choices.

Finally, Friedberg and Webb (2006) explicitly link the bargaining model approach to time use research. They argue that relative wages are a good proxy for bargaining power within the household in determining the spousal household production split. They find significant effects of the relative wage only on weekend television watching and house cleaning, but even these statistically significant effects are small. Our paper differs from Friedberg and Webb's in that we include weekdays as well as weekends, and we control for weekly hours of employment. Our results, however, are consistent with theirs as we find no effects of relative wages on the wife's time use patterns in our broad categories of leisure, caregiving, and home production.

THEORETICAL UNDERPINNINGS AND EQUATION SPECIFICATION

Our underlying utility-maximizing framework extends the model used in the previous chapter to include spousal time inputs in nonmarket production of goods and services, including child services, and permits the potential complementarity of joint leisure time.[5] Mothers are still modeled as allocating their time among five choices: paid work, unpaid household production, caregiving, leisure, and other activities.[6] However, in the model in Chapter 3, there is no explicit role for the mother's husband except that his very presence and his monthly earnings exogenously affect the budget constraint. For this chapter, we modify the model so that the mother maximizes her utility over her leisure time and her husband's leisure time, adult goods, and child services subject to a series of production functions and constraints. The husband's leisure appears in the mother's utility function to account for the potential complementarity of jointly consumed leisure time. Both adult goods and child services are produced with a combination of each parent's time and purchased market goods (see Appendix D).

The maximization of the mother's utility function subject to her money budget constraint, her time constraint, his time constraint, the child's time constraint, and the two production functions yields three unpaid time use demand equations of the form:

$$t_j = f(E_m, E_f \mid D, S) \text{ for } j = \text{household production, caregiving, and leisure.}$$

In the above equation, E_m denotes economic factors of the mother, E_f denotes economic factors of her husband (the father), D denotes demographic factors, and S denotes timing and spatial factors. We estimate these three time use functions in a simultaneous system estimated via Seemingly Unrelated Regression Tobit.[7]

The demographic and timing and spatial controls included as D and S are identical to those used in Chapter 3. The economic factors used in this chapter are expanded from the previous chapter, including additional factors for the mother as well as economic factors relating to the husband. The mother's economic factors include her predicted hourly wage, predicted usual weekly employment hours, and two predicted child care prices identical to those already discussed in Chapter 3.[8] Note that the mother's predicted hourly wage appears in the model in two ways: first, directly, as was done in the previous chapter, and then as a component in the calculated relative wage; i.e., the wife's wage divided by the husband's wage. We use this relative wage measure, which is the one preferred by Pollak (2005), because it controls for spousal potential income and its marginal effects can be interpreted as a change in one's own "power" within the couple. Other things equal, the greater the power that the wife exerts in household decision making, the more sharing of household production time within couples is expected. Thus, we expect a higher relative wage to reduce the mother's home production time and to increase her leisure time. The effect on caregiving time is ambiguous theoretically as it depends on how the mother chooses to spend her power—she may choose to use her power to have more or less time with the children.

The full household decision-making process modeled above implies that a husband or wife's time in an activity is affected by the other's time spent in that same activity. It could be that the husband and wife divide up a fixed set of tasks or that more time spent cleaning by the wife means that the husband also is expected to clean more. In either case, empirically, we examine the wife's time devoted to household production, for example, while controlling for the husband's engagement in home production.

In addition to the husband's time use in the same activity, we include the price of his time (i.e., his hourly wage), which is incorporated into the model in the form of the denominator of the relative wage as described above, and the husband's usual weekly employment hours, which is the largest and more inflexible component of the underlying time constraint in time use decision making. Usual weekly employment hours and hourly wage rates of the husband are available in the Current Population Survey data file that is attached to the mother's ATUS time diary data.[9] However, the husband's time devoted to the same activity requires time diary information and is not available in the ATUS because, by survey design, only one adult per household is administered the time use survey. Thus, although we have a great deal of demographic information about spouses, we lack the detailed time use information for the same day for the spouse—a crucial piece of information for the study of couples' joint time use.

Although actual spousal diaries are not available in the ATUS, we do have time diaries from men who are married to mothers of young children. We know a great deal about these men: we know their age, education, race, ethnicity, number of coresident children, and usual hours worked. Using this information, we can construct predicted husband's time use from the men's time diaries provided in the ATUS. This "out-of-sample" strategy has both pros and cons for our purposes. One advantage is that this methodology is familiar to many readers; it is a variant of the strategy that is usually used to construct wages for non-workers, which was described in the previous chapter. In this case, we use a sample of married fathers' ATUS time diaries and estimate reduced form Tobit regression equations for each of the three nonpaid time uses using characteristics of the father and his wife as regressors. We then calculate predicted husbands' time in the activity for each mother in our mothers' sample, using the estimated coefficients from the reduced form Tobit regression equations and the observed characteristics of the actual mother and spouse. A second advantage of this strategy is that it uses the full sample of observations in order to estimate the coefficients of the determinants of time spent on the three nonpaid activities and the actual husband's characteristics exactly. The disadvantage is that the correlation among the three time uses of the husband are lost since each is a predicted value based on estimated coefficients. In addition, all the covariance between mothers' and fathers' time is missing since the fathers' time use is estimated from observable characteristics only.[10]

At first glance, the "out-of-sample" data construction strategy appears to be a second-best solution, where the "best" strategy would be to rely on observed time use diaries for the husband (although that strategy is not an option using the ATUS). However, the use of the actual spouse's time use may not even be the desirable approach. If actual husband's time use is jointly determined with mother's time use, as the model predicts, using the actual husband's time in the same activity could lead to endogeneity bias in the estimated marginal effects (see Connelly and Kimmel 2009a). One solution to this endogeneity problem would be to use the same "out-of-sample" prediction technique that we use in this chapter to construct predicted measures of spousal time. Thus, the out-of-sample prediction technique might be used even if we could observe the actual time use of husbands.

MOTHERS' NONMARKET TIME USE PATTERNS

Our estimating samples yield 2,370 mothers with weekday diaries and 2,661 with weekend diaries. Recall that in this chapter we are focusing on three types of unpaid time: household production time, child caregiving time, and leisure. Table 4.1 shows the total minutes devoted to the three unpaid activities reported on the ATUS time use survey files for married mothers for both weekdays and weekends. Corresponding figures for average minutes in each activity for their husbands are constructed using the out-of-sample prediction method discussed above.

Table 4.1 Average Minutes in Unpaid Time Uses for Married Mothers

	Active leisure	Child caregiving	Home production
Weekdays			
Married mothers	272.46	160.80	217.23
	(154.42)	(135.63)	(163.10)
Husbands of married mothers	284.59	38.17	71.51
Sample size = 2,370	(33.42)	(44.64)	(23.18)
Weekends			
Married mothers	403.78	109.53	265.87
	(186.27)	(127.68)	(170.40)
Husbands of married mothers	468.01	37.73	187.80
Sample size = 2,661	(36.83)	(44.13)	(25.75)

NOTE: Standard deviations are in parentheses.
SOURCE: ATUS 2003–2006, unweighted.

In interpreting Table 4.1, it is useful to recall the finding from the previous chapters that paid work time for both husbands and wives falls from weekdays to weekend days. Thus, on weekends a large amount of time is freed up for unpaid activities. For mothers, note that the average number of minutes devoted to leisure increases on the weekend, as does unpaid household work time (we see this in Figures 2.1 and 2.2). However, caregiving time falls on the weekends, as is noted in the previous chapters. What is new in Table 4.1 is the information reported for husbands. Looking at husbands' leisure time, there appears to be an increase in leisure time from weekdays to weekend days. However, for caregiving, there is no substantive difference between weekdays and weekends. Finally, for husbands' unpaid household production, there is an increase in time devoted to household production on the weekends.

Average values for the additional economic factors are shown in Table 4.2. Married mothers of children under age 13 earn on average 65 percent of their husbands' hourly wages. On average, the husband usually works approximately 40 hours per week, while the mothers typically have about 13 hours of paid work per week.

Table 4.2 Average Values of Additional Economic Factors to Be Included in the Multivariate Analysis

	Relative wage % (Mothers' predicted wage/husbands' predicted wage)	Husband's predicted weekly work hours	Own predicted weekly work hours
Weekdays	65	40.89	13.81
	(0.17)	(4.02)	(8.84)
Weekends	65	40.76	13.53
	(0.18)	(3.95)	(8.85)

NOTE: Standard deviations are in parentheses.
SOURCE: ATUS 2003–2006, unweighted.

REGRESSION FINDINGS

We focus our discussion here on the key factors that distinguish this chapter's empirical work from the previous chapter.[11] Table 4.3 presents the marginal effects of the mother's own economic factors on her time choices. These results include the effects of her wage, the two prices of child care, and her usual weekly employment hours. The positive effect of own wages on caregiving hours is robust to expansion of the model in this chapter to include husband's characteristics and to limiting of the sample to married mothers. The inclusion of usual work hours is new in this model. We find that on weekdays, the wife's own usual work hours is related negatively to both her primary child caregiving time and her household production, suggesting trade-offs between employment and these two activities during the week. On weekends, only caregiving is related negatively to usual paid work hours. Note that leisure time is not related significantly to usual paid work hours on weekdays nor on weekends.

Table 4.4 presents the results of the economic factors relating to the husband, including the relative wage, the husband's usual weekly work hours, and the husband's minutes in the same time category. As noted above, we define the relative wage as the predicted wage of the wife divided by the predicted wage of the husband. Table 4.4 shows that in each of the nonpaid time use categories, the relative wage has no effect on mothers' time use choices. The lack of significant effects of the relative wage on household production time is particularly interesting given the evidence from past studies that relative income did affect household production time. However, our econometric specification, our inclusion of nonemployed mothers, and the time period from which our data are drawn differ substantially enough from past studies that differences in the findings are to be expected.

We find that husbands' usual weekly employment hours play no role in mothers' leisure time choices but do affect both her caregiving (positively) and household production time choices (negatively) on weekdays. The finding that the husbands' usual weekly work hours are positively associated with the mother's caregiving time is consistent with Hallberg and Klevmarken (2003), who show that for dual-earning couples in Sweden, additional work time for fathers increased mothers' caregiving time. The effect of husbands' employment time on weekday household production is just the opposite; that is, the greater the husband's usual time devoted to paid work, the lower the wife's time spent on weekday household production. Chapter 3 tells us that the presence of a husband increased home production time of women, but here we find that if he is home less, fewer minutes are devoted to home production. On weekends, none of the mother's unpaid time uses are affected by her husband's usual weekly employment time. This is consistent with the notion that fathers' intensity in paid work is heavier on weekdays, and thus imposes more of a family time constraint.

Recall that spousal time use in the same time category is unavailable directly in the ATUS, thus it required prediction. Husbands' leisure time is shown to increase mothers' leisure time on weekdays but to decrease their leisure time on weekends. These results indicate that based on observables, mothers whose husbands have more leisure time also have more leisure time on weekdays, perhaps because they are spending leisure time together. However, on weekends, mothers with husbands who have more leisure minutes tend to have fewer minutes of leisure themselves. This may be because leisure and caregiving are more fluid on the weekends, so that if he is playing golf, she is driving kids to soccer.[12]

Regarding caregiving, we find some evidence of the complementarity of spousal caregiving time with the result that couples' caregiving time moves jointly on weekdays.[13] These findings are consistent with

Table 4.3 Marginal Effects of Own Economic Factors on Mothers' Unpaid Time Use

	Weekdays				Weekends			
	Own wage	Own usual weekly work hours	Price of child care 0–5	Price of child care 6–12	Own wage	Own usual weekly work hours	Price of child care 0–5	Price of child care 6–12
Leisure	−17.4202	−0.9704	−1.3366	4.4582*	−80.9876	−0.2831	−2.9968	4.9359*
Caregiving	72.4938*	−1.4654*	5.4637***	−0.1582	54.7251***	−1.0786***	2.0271**	−3.2074***
Home prod.	4.3381	−3.0068***	1.2804	1.1827	54.6334	1.2785	2.0458	2.9354

NOTE: Marginal effects for the time in caregiving and time in home production were calculated at the means values of the variables. Leisure was estimated OLS so that the coefficients are the marginal effects. *significant at the 0.10 level; **significant at the 0.05 level; ***significant at the 0.01 level.

SOURCE: ATUS 2003–2006.

Table 4.4 Marginal Effects of Husbands' Economic Factors on Mothers' Unpaid Time Use

	Weekdays			Weekend		
	Relative wage	Husbands' usual weekly work hours	Husbands' minutes in same time category	Relative wage	Husbands' usual weekly work hours	Husbands' minutes in same time category
Leisure	−74.5375	−1.3324	0.7179***	3.2051	−0.5083	−0.3039***
Caregiving	33.3749	2.7830*	0.2585*	−4.5001	0.9450	−0.1092
Home prod.	−12.0050	−3.3699**	−0.1197	−27.4181	−1.4129	0.2934*

NOTE: Marginal effects for the time in caregiving and time in household production were calculated at the means values of the variables. Time in leisure was estimated using ordinary least squares so that the coefficients are the marginal effects.
*significant at the 0.10 level; **significant at the 0.05 level; ***significant at the 0.01 level.
SOURCE: ATUS 2003–2006.

Hallberg and Klevmarken (2003), who find that the caregiving time of Swedish husbands and wives were complementary. Complementarity of parental caregiving time implies that the gap in parental attention to children by wage level is even greater than it appears in Chapter 3. Higher-wage mothers spend more time with their children on both weekdays and weekends and are married to men who also spend more time with their children, and the more time one parent spends with the children, the more time the other spends with the children.[14]

Finally, turning to household production, the only statistically significant finding is seen on weekends. Here, mothers' and fathers' household production time moves jointly, suggesting either that the fungibility of housework drives both spouses' time choices or that assortative mating is a driving factor in weekend home production time (i.e., neater men marry neater women and they jointly desire neater houses).

CONCLUSION

This chapter has focused on the effect that husbands' economic variables have on mothers' time use in three aggregated nonpaid time categories: leisure, caregiving, and household production. One important result is the finding that relative wages have no significant effect on any of mothers' nonmarket time use choices.[15] This result is somewhat surprising because of past studies of household production, but those results usually came from relative income instead of relative wages and often were constrained to dual-earner couples. Our result is consistent with the results of Friedberg and Webb (2006), who use the same ATUS data and a similar definition of relative wages, and who also find no effect of relative wages on weekend time use of women (except for the narrow time categories of television watching and house cleaning).[16] It may be that relative wages are not proxying for power within the household, or that power within the household is not manifest in time spent in aggregate time categories in systematic ways. We are inclined to believe the latter hypotheses but will leave it to future research to sort through the various alternative hypotheses.

The weekly employment time of the husband (and the mothers' own employment time as well) is an important determinant of mothers' weekday caregiving and household production time. We have argued throughout the book that caregiving time is less fungible than leisure or household production, and that hypothesis is supported with these results. If the husband is working more hours, then the mother is providing more weekday caregiving. Her own weekly employment hours negatively affect her caregiving time on both weekdays and weekends.

The somewhat surprising result is the finding that the husband's weekly employment hours are related negatively to the mother's weekday household production time. This is further evidence of the elective nature of home production. At a minimum, it is consistent with the popularly held notion that if the father is not home for dinner, the mother does not bother to cook. Alternatively, the ultimate daily time constraint may mean that if Mom is in charge of baths for the children, then she is not doing the laundry. The magnitude of the effect is smaller on the weekend, consistent with the notion that time is more flexible on the weekend.

Finally, concerning the spouse's time use in the same activity, we find some significant effects. Husbands' time in home production seems to be a complement for mothers' weekend housework time, and husbands' caregiving time seems to complement mothers' caregiving time on weekdays. Finally, weekday leisure appears complementary, while the effect of increased husbands' leisure is negative on mothers' weekend leisure. The sum of these results is consistent with previous research that showed that the gains from marriage coming from specialization have declined since the 1960s (Lundberg and Pollak 2007). As gains from complementarities increase in importance, we would expect more positive assortative mating, which would reinforce further the observation of complementary uses of time.

What has this analysis added to our understanding of caregiving time? Table 4.3 shows that there remain strong predictions of positive wage effects on caregiving time for this sample of married women, even when spousal economic characteristics are controlled. Higher-wage married mothers spend more time on caregiving, and Table 4.4 tells us that the more time they spend on caregiving, the more time their husbands spend on caregiving, leading to a substantial time gap between time devoted to young children across wage groups. More research is needed about the gaps in individual components of child caregiving time and whether the gap is enhanced or dissipated by a more inclusive definition of caregiving time. Finally, this chapter provides encouragement to researchers seeking to study couples' time use using the ATUS by offering an empirical strategy for overcoming the single diary per household constraint.

Notes

1. Hallberg and Klevmarken (2003) find evidence of complementarity in Swedish parents' caregiving time.
2. Models related to the power in the marriage relationship stem from the divorce threat point model (McElroy and Horney 1981), the collective framework models of Chiappori and colleagues (Chiappori 1988; Browning and Chiappori 1998; and Chiappori, Fortin, and Lacroix 2002), or in the separate spheres threat point of Lundberg and Pollak (1993). Empirical work based on these bargaining models has confirmed the relevance of a bargaining approach in understanding joint labor supply. Pollak (2005) argues that relative wage is a better measure of power than relative earnings when home production is important.
3. For examples of empirical evidence on gender differences in unpaid home production time both in the United States and internationally, see Alvarez and Miles (2003), Bittman et al. (2003), Hersch and Stratton (2002), and Sousa-Poza, Schmid, and Widmer (2001). Recall in the previous chapter that we find strong positive effects of marriage on home production time for mothers on both weekdays and weekends.
4. Projecting these results to the present is difficult, as one suspects that results from data collected 30 years ago may be different from those generated by more recent data because of the substantial changes in the labor supply of married women.
5. Our model is also similar to Hallberg and Klevmarken (2003), except we model home production and leisure time along with caregiving time. The full model derivation is presented in Appendix D.
6. For our measure of leisure, we exclude time spent sleeping or engaging in personal care. See Chapter 3 and Aguiar and Hurst (2007) for further elaboration on the definition of leisure.
7. Although our focus is nonpaid time use, the interaction between employment time and nonpaid time is too great to ignore. The estimation in Chapter 3 finds substantial correlations between employment and each of the three nonpaid time uses on both weekdays and weekends. In this chapter, predicted usual weekly employment time is included as a determinant of nonpaid time.
8. This measure of usual weekly work hours is predicted from a preliminary regression. Employment time clearly is in competition with nonpaid time. Since many nonpaid activities are fungible across the week, weekly employment hours are preferable for estimation purposes to diary day employment hours.

9. Note, however, that the CPS employment data have a four- to five-month time lag with the ATUS data, so for some fathers, their employment may have changed between the timing of the two surveys.

10. Connelly and Kimmel (2009b) contrast the out-of-sample prediction presented here with an alternative prediction strategy that uses propensity matching. We decided to present the out-of-sample prediction strategy here based on those results and from German Time Use data presented in Connelly and Kimmel (2009a).

11. Note that the demographic and spatial factors are the same as those included in the previous chapter's regressions, and the findings here are consistent with those earlier results. Also, own wages and the prices of child care effects are very similar to those reported in Chapter 3. Importantly, the own-wage effect on child care time continues to be positive on both weekdays and weekends. Note that our sample here is limited to married mothers, while the sample in Chapter 3 includes both married and unmarried mothers.

12. Ramey and Ramey (2008) show that child care time has increased in the United States over the past 40 years and that much of the increase is attributable to driving older children to and from various activities.

13. See Bianchi et al. (2006, Chapter 6) for direct evidence on the correlation of mothers' and fathers' time with children.

14. We show that high-wage fathers spend more time with children in Connelly and Kimmel (2009b).

15. This result is robust to many changes in the specifications of the three time use equations. It was true when the spouse's predicted time in the same activity is excluded, as reported in Connelly and Kimmel (2008).

16. As was described earlier in this chapter, our work differs from that of Friedberg and Webb in several important ways.

5

The Role of Nonstandard Work Hours in Maternal Caregiving

In our analysis of mothers' time use, we have concentrated on the total minutes of time devoted to aggregated time categories. In Chapter 3, one of the four aggregate time categories considered is employment time on the diary day. In Chapter 4, employment time again plays a role, but it is weekly employment time that is posited to affect the allocation of daily time for child caregiving, home production, and leisure. In this chapter, we think again about employment time's effect on caregiving, but here our concern is how the time of day of paid work affects a mother's allocation of time to child caregiving.

We provided some descriptive evidence concerning the timing of caregiving in Chapter 2. Figures 2.16 and 2.17 provide evidence of the fluctuation in the incidence of caregiving across a 24-hour period. In those figures, we record the percentage of mothers engaged in child caregiving activities at each hour of the day. A similar pattern of caregiving timing is seen across different groups of mothers, by age of the youngest child and weekend versus weekday. In each graph there is a peak in the percentage of mothers engaged in caregiving around 8 a.m. and again between 6 and 8 p.m. The peak is more pronounced on weekdays than weekends and most pronounced for young school-aged children. Figures 2.18 and 2.19 contrast the group of mothers with children aged 0–5 who are employed full time during the week to those not employed. The same bimodal pattern of caregiving time can be seen for both groups, though it is more pronounced for those employed full time. But how much does the time of day of employment affect the mother's caregiving time choices? This is the topic we explore in this chapter.

Researchers are interested in the incidence of nonstandard work, that is, employment at times other than Monday through Friday "standard hours," for a variety of reasons. First, nonstandard work affects a significant proportion of today's workers and their families. Second, working outside the traditional weekday work schedule may place an additional burden on individuals and families. According to Presser (2004, p. 1), "Research suggests that such schedules undermine the stability of marriages, increase the amount of housework to be done, reduce family cohesiveness, and require elaborate child-care arrangements."[1] According to Collins et al. (2000) in *The National Study of Child Care for Low-Income Families*, shortages in child care slots available during nonstandard working hours are often reported by lower-income mothers. Additionally, nonstandard work can make it difficult for parents to have dinner with their children or to supervise homework. Polivka (2008) and Wight, Raley, and Bianchi (2008) show that nonstandard working married partners enjoy less time alone with their spouses. Disruption of sleep patterns can have adverse health effects, and performing shift work raises the risk of on-the-job injury (Fortson 2004). There also may be negative effects of parents' nonstandard work on their children (Han 2005).

In this chapter, we consider whether mothers who are employed any hours outside the traditional 8 a.m. to 6 p.m. workday (i.e., nonstandard work hours) on their diary day differ in their caregiving behavior. We also look at how morning work hours affect morning caregiving hours and how evening work hours affect evening caregiving hours. Of course, working standard versus nonstandard hours is, in part, a choice, and so we model the simultaneity of the choice of time spent with children and the choice of employment schedule. The methodology we use is an endogenous switching regression in which we estimate the probability of working nonstandard hours simultaneously with the hours spent on child caregiving activities during the 24-hour diary day.

Recall that the ATUS contains only one day's worth of time use information. For many analyses, such as those in Chapters 3 and 4, having only one day is somewhat problematic. We worry about chores being moved across the week to compensate for today's time constraints. However, for the issue we are considering here, we have exactly the information we need: the interrelationships between time choices made on a particular day. In other words, we can answer the following question: If a mother worked late yesterday, did she spend less time, on average, with her children than she would have had she not worked late?

NONSTANDARD EMPLOYMENT AND ITS IMPLICATIONS FOR CAREGIVING

Nonstandard work is an important and growing phenomenon in the American workplace.[2] The incidence of nonstandard employment depends on how it is measured. The CPS asks about the usual weekly work schedule. Focusing just on full-time wage and salary workers, the percentage reporting nonstandard schedules has ranged from 14 to 18 percent for the past 30 years. While industrialization in the early 1900s was credited with the early advent of nonstandard work, more recently, the rise of female paid employment and the increasing demand for service workers has been associated with continued relatively high rates of nonstandard work (BLS 2005; Hedges and Sekscenski 1979; Polivka 2008; Presser 2003).

Presser (2003) claims that structural labor demand shifts as well as the evolution of societal norms have contributed to the increase in nonstandard jobs. According to Beers (2000) and BLS (2005), the majority (51 percent) of nonstandard workers do not appear to be working these times due to personal choice but instead "due to the nature of the job." Presumably, the other 49 percent have chosen (to some extent) their nonstandard schedules. Eight percent report taking such jobs to accommodate family responsibilities. Nonstandard paid work hours of one parent can reduce the amount of nonparental child care used. Why else might a worker choose to work nonstandard hours? Presser (2003) lists several such reasons, including a possible pay premium, less managerial supervision, or an easier commute. In addition, mothers may have preferences regarding the particular time of day that they engage in caregiving. For example, some mothers place greater importance on being home when their children return from school. This is consistent with the findings of Venn (2004), who finds a preference on the part of Australian mothers for caregiving in the early morning hours as well as directly after school.

Kimmel and Powell (2006a,b) examine the impact of nonstandard work on the child care modal choices of married and single mothers, respectively. They find that nonstandard employed mothers are less likely to report paying for child care (37 percent versus 68 percent for those mothers working standard hours). Their regression results reveal that even when the endogeneity of nonstandard work is considered, mothers who work nonstandard hours are significantly less likely to utilize formal modes of care (i.e., center care or sitter care), probably because of the time inflexibility of these modes of care. As Kimmel and Powell (2006b) explain, the implications of nonstandard work are particularly acute for single mothers, both due to their proportionately higher incidence of such work (due to their relatively low educational attainment) and the limited availability of relative care or father care, the modes of care preferred by nonstandard working mothers.[3]

Two papers use time diary data to expand our knowledge of the relationship between employment timing and parental caregiving. Wight, Raley, and Bianchi (2008) examine the role of work-time scheduling on time devoted to family and self. Using data from the ATUS (but without any treatment of the endogeneity of nonstandard work), they find that nonstandard work does not necessarily reduce parents' time with children. In fact, for mothers working mostly night hours, and fathers working evening or night hours, time spent with children is greater. One downside of parental nonstandard work is that time with the spouse is reduced, as is own personal time. Another apparent downside is that mothers of school-aged children report less involvement with their children's educational activities.

The research most similar to the work presented in this chapter is that of Rapoport and Le Bourdais (2008), who study the role that nonstandard work schedules play in parental time choices for Canadian parents. They find that the strongest effects of employment hours on parental time with children result from nonstandard work during the evening; specifically, the effect is largest on leisure and social activities with children.

CHOOSING CAREGIVING MINUTES WITH A CONSIDERATION FOR SCHEDULES

The standard labor/leisure model is often used to describe the allocation of an individual's time between employment and leisure. In that model, all possible paid work hours are valued at the same hourly wage rate, and the marginal hour of leisure is valued at the same level regardless of the time of day at which it occurs. Winston (1982) offers a more complex model of time use that differs from the standard labor/ leisure model in that the time of day of the hour of leisure or the hour of employment affects the marginal valuation of time. More recently, Hamermesh (1996, 1999) offers a simplified version of the Winston model, showing that the choice to perform paid work at any specific point in the day depends on the time-dependent marginal rate of substitution of consumption for leisure time and the time-varying wage rate.[4] The marginal rate of substitution is expected to vary across individuals who differ in marital status and the presence of children of various ages.

As we have already argued in Chapter 3, the standard labor/leisure model needs to be expanded to incorporate additional aggregate time uses; particularly, we have argued that we need to separate caregiving time from home production time. The empirical evidence offered in Chapter 3 makes it clear that caregiving time is distinct from other unpaid household production and from leisure. Given the importance placed on caregiving time, it is critical to note other ways that the standard model might be improved for mothers of young children. The most important consideration is that mothers face a child's time constraint as well as their own time constraints. The child's time constraint reflects the fact that young children must be cared for by someone 24 hours a day (Connelly 1992). Since most paid work is incompatible with simultaneously caring for young children, an hour of maternal employment requires that someone other than the mother take responsibility for the child during that hour. The alternative caregiver may be the mother's spouse, another member of the household, a relative or friend from outside the household, formal child care, or elementary school. Some of these caregivers charge a fee for their services, affecting the net wage rate the mother earns from employment. In addition, since we are interested in the time of day of labor and leisure, the availability of these alternative caregivers and in some cases price is also a function of the time of day.

Institutional modes of nonmaternal care have varying degrees of time flexibility. Child care centers almost always operate during daytime hours only, though some may open as early as 6 a.m. to accommodate early morning work starting times. In addition, centers usually sell their services by the day of the week in full or half days, making it difficult to accommodate work schedules that change week to week.

Family day care usually is more flexible than center-based care but still mainly operates at times compatible with standard work schedules. Elementary schools have hours that are both the most inflexible and the least accommodating to employment, operating from 8 or 9 a.m. until 2 or 3 p.m. Additionally, many communities still offer only half-day kindergarten.[5] The school year also has many more vacation days than employees receive and often has late starts or early release days, all of which exacerbate the work/family conflict faced by parents.

In the United States, the child care used to accommodate nonstandard work hours overwhelmingly is father and other relative care (Han 2004; Kimmel and Powell 2006a,b; Presser 2003). This is clearly the result of both the increased availability of fathers and relatives at these nonstandard work times and the unavailability of formal child care. What is not clear is which effect is the dominant one. For some couples, nonstandard work hours are chosen specifically to minimize nonparental child care hours. In fact, it is thought that this "tag-teaming" can increase fathers' involvement with their children (Casper and O'Connell 1998; Presser 1988; Wight, Raley, and Bianchi 2008). However, we don't know whether the hours that fathers spend with their children substitute for formal child care hours only or also substitute for the mother's time. In other words, it is possible that a mother's time with her children could be unaffected by working nonstandard versus standard hours if care by the father or other relatives is only used during paid employment hours and completely substitutes for formal child care time.

The possibility that a mother's time with children is unaffected by working nonstandard hours seems unlikely given the constraints imposed by school hours and normal bedtimes. Women who begin paid work before the child wakes up will not put in any minutes of caregiving before school. Women who are engaged in paid work away from their home during their children's bedtime routine will not record any minutes in caregiving in the evening. On the other hand, women who work in the evening may be home when their children come home from school, and thus may report some caregiving minutes during this after-school time. Presser (2003) finds that employed mothers of children ages 5–11 who work the evening or night shift are significantly more likely to report always or usually being home before and after school (pp. 195–196). Clearly, mothers' preferences regarding their caregiving time vary, and the timing of paid employment plays a complex role in the distribution of this caregiving.

A final concern related to the linkage between mothers' time choices and their children's care time constraint is that parents' work schedules can also affect their children's schedules. Research from Australia shows that single parents of young children start their days earlier and end their days later than married parents (Craig 2007). This is one of the ways that mothers protect time with their children from their increased hours of employment.

FURTHER DESCRIPTIVE STATISTICS CONCERNING CAREGIVING AND NONSTANDARD EMPLOYMENT

Our sample in this chapter is limited to mothers who report paid work hours at some point in their weekday diary day since our interest is in the interaction between employment hours on a given day and caregiving hours on the same day.[6] This criterion, along with the requirement that each mother have information on her husband's (or partner's) wage if she is married or cohabiting, leads to a sample size of 1,894 women.

Table 5.1 shows the average caregiving and employment minutes for mothers with positive employment hours on the diary day. In this table and throughout the chapter, we categorize the mothers as nonstandard workers if they report that they performed *any* of their paid work minutes on the diary day outside of "standard work hours" that we define as 8 a.m. to 6 p.m. Under this definition, 58 percent of our sample of mothers with positive employment hours on the diary day worked some of those hours after 6 p.m. or before 8 a.m. Of the minutes employed on diary day for mothers with any nonstandard hours, 23 percent of their work time occurs during the nonstandard hours. Ten percent occurs during the early morning hours of 5 a.m. to 8 a.m., a time when mothers may encounter binding children's time constraints due to the necessity of performing tasks associated with waking and preparing children for school or day care. Eleven percent of the nonstandard working mothers' paid work minutes, on average, occur during the evening hours of 6 p.m. to midnight, prime time for dinner, homework, and

**Table 5.1 Average Caregiving and Employment Minutes for Mothers
with Positive Employment Hours on the Diary Day**

	Standard employment hours only	Any nonstandard employment hours	Significant difference
Sample size	801	1,093	
Percent of total sample	42.3	57.7	
Minutes employed/time of day			
Total	363.4	484.4	***
Early morning	0	43.7	***
Standard day	363.4	379.3	**
Evening	0	50.5	***
Nighttime	0	11.0	***
Minutes spent caregiving/time of day			
Total	126.8	95.2	***
Early morning	27.3	18.8	***
Standard	46.7	34.8	***
Evening	49.7	38.1	***
Nighttime	3.1	3.5	

NOTE: Asterisks represent results of t-test of means across employment hours categories. **significant at the 0.05 level; ***significant at the 0.01 level.
SOURCE: ATUS 2003–2006, unweighted.

bedtime routines. Only 3 percent, on average, of the paid work time of nonstandard workers occurs overnight from midnight to 5 a.m.

Most other researchers have used a more stringent definition of nonstandard workers. Presser (2003) defines nonstandard workers as those who work "most" (i.e., over half) of their hours at nonstandard times because "doing so more sharply differentiates people who organize their lives around one predominant work schedule." However, she notes that "the prevalence rate for nonstandard hours would be much higher if those working 'some' late hours were included" (p. 14). Similarly, Polivka (2008) and Wight, Raley, and Bianchi (2008), using ATUS data, define workers as nonstandard if more than half of the hours are at times other than weekdays between the more narrowly defined hours of 8 a.m. and 4 p.m. Note that our range of hours is longer to reflect the availability of formal day care beyond 4 p.m. However, more importantly, the criteria we are using is *any* hours outside the range, not the majority of hours outside the range. When we use Polivka's more re-strictive nonstandard work categorization, 11 percent of the estimation sample would be classified as nonstandard. This number is in line with Polivka's results. While Presser undoubtedly is right that working the majority of one's hours at nonstandard times means one must organize one's life in a different way, *any* minutes a parent with young children works at a nonstandard time represents an incompatibility with start-ing or ending times of formal day care, or elementary school, and the normal rhythms of a child's sleep. Consequently, *any* nonstandard time must be dealt with through alternative arrangements. Since the ATUS provides only one diary day per person, we prefer the *any* nonstandard hours criterion for identifying the nonstandard worker when the focus is analyzing the effect of being employed at nonstandard times on moth-ers' caregiving time on that same day. However, we did run a sensitivity analysis by using Polivka's definition of the majority of hours being nonstandard to determine the importance of the nonstandard definition to our results. For a comparison of the results see Connelly and Kimmel (forthcoming).

Table 5.1 shows the mean values for caregiving and employment time of the sample stratified by whether the mother was employed any nonstandard minutes on the weekday diary day. Nonstandard workers work substantially more total minutes on the diary day, approximately 8 hours (484 minutes) compared to approximately 6 hours for the stan-dard hours only sample. Note that the average employment time just during standard hours is approximately the same for the two samples.[7] However, while nonstandard workers report working for pay on the di-ary day on average two hours more, they only spent 32 fewer minutes on caregiving activities on the diary day. This suggests that most of maternal caregiving time is preserved by nonstandard working mothers.

What is the distribution of caregiving across the diary day and how does this distribution vary by work status? Figure 5.1 records the percent of mothers engaged in caregiving as each hour strikes, just as previously shown in Figures 2.16–2.19, but here the sample is divided by whether the employed mother worked any nonstandard hours. Fig-ure 5.1 shows that while the caregiving for mothers employed only standard hours is bimodal (caregiving occurs before and after standard employment hours), the caregiving time of mothers employed non-standard hours is distributed more evenly throughout the day, although

Figure 5.1 Percent of Mothers with Any Nonstandard Employment Hours or No Nonstandard Employment Hours Engaged in Child Caregiving, by Hour of the Diary Day

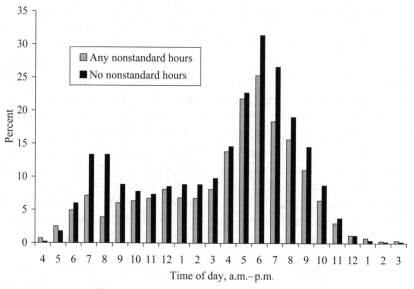

still with a peak in the late afternoon and early evening. In addition, a smaller percentage of mothers working nonstandard hours are engaged in caregiving at any time of the day.

Table 5.2 presents the means of variables used in our multivariate child caregiving time models.[8] We do not find many statistically significant differences between workers with only standard hours versus those with some nonstandard hours. The variables that have significantly different means (based on a standard t-test) between the two samples are education (13.9 years for nonstandard workers versus 14.3 years for standard workers); husbands' monthly earnings ($2,359 versus $2,640); urban residence (71 percent versus 76 percent); the presence of other adults (16 percent versus 11 percent); the predicted hourly wage (in natural logarithm; 2.40 an hour versus 2.45 an hour); the predicted price of child care for children aged 6–12 ($2.14 an hour versus $2.34 an hour); and predicted weekly employment hours (36.0 hours versus 35.6 hours). Note that nonstandard workers also have fewer 6–9-year-olds (0.52 versus 0.57) with a p-value = 0.109. It is important to remember

Table 5.2 Sample Means for Regression Covariates

	Any nonstandard employment hours	Standard employment hours only	Significant difference
Education	13.9012	14.2797	***
Age	35.5087	35.8065	
Husband's monthly earnings if married (in thousands of dollars)	2.3594	2.6398	**
Married	0.6240	0.6267	
Nonwhite	0.1921	0.1735	
Hispanic	0.1491	0.1323	
Urban	0.7100	0.7603	**
South	0.3586	0.3396	
No. of children aged 0–2	0.2626	0.2684	
No. of children aged 3–5	0.3202	0.3296	
No. of children aged 6–9	0.5197	0.5680	
No. of children aged 10–12	0.4575	0.4432	
No. of children aged 13–17	0.2772	0.2672	
Presence of other adult in household	0.1555	0.1099	***
Summer	0.2608	0.2484	
Predicted ln hourly wage	2.3997	2.4523	***
Predicted hourly price of child care for a 0–5-year-old	2.3719	2.4427	
Predicted hourly price of child care for a 6–12-year-old	2.1361	2.3387	**
Predicted weekly employment hours	36.0053	35.6266	***
N	1,093	801	

NOTE: The sample includes all mothers with children less than 13 years old who have positive hours of paid employment on a weekday diary day and data in all right-hand-side variables. Asterisks represent results of t-test of means across employment hours categories. **significant at the 0.05 level; ***significant at the 0.01 level.
SOURCE: ATUS 2003–2006, unweighted.

that studies that use the more stringent definition of nonstandard workers—workers whose majority of employment time is during nonstandard hours (though the hour range is more narrowly defined)—report substantial differences in the characteristics of nonstandard and standard hour workers, with nonstandard workers having lower levels of education and work experience (see Connelly and Kimmel [forthcoming]).

It is interesting that the mothers who work only standard hours have more 6–9-year-old children than the mothers employed some nonstandard hours. These young school-aged children represent the group with the most binding time of day constraints; they need to be at school at a certain time, they need to be picked up from school at a certain time, and they are seldom left at home alone before or after school. Mothers who work only standard hours also have a higher average wage than those who work some nonstandard hours. Typically, nonstandard work is lower-skill employment, with a disproportionate percentage of jobs in the service sector. However, based on our definition of *any* nonstandard hours on the diary day, our sample also includes higher paid women workers who happen to be working late on the diary day. Probably for this reason, while statistically significant, the difference in wages between to the two samples is very modest.

EMPIRICAL MODEL

The time of day that one engages in paid work is itself a choice, at least for some women.[9] Some mothers specifically want to be home when their children return from school. These mothers may choose to work early in the morning or evenings to ensure they are available for their children in the middle of the afternoon. Similarly, those who value the time with their children before school will try to avoid early morning employment hours. In order to account for the possibility that nonstandard hours decisions are made jointly with child caregiving time decisions, we implement an endogenous switching model, sometimes referred to as a mover/stayer model. The specification allows the role of caregiving time to be different for those mothers working nonstandard hours and those working standard hours. The determinants of working any nonstandard hours are estimated jointly with the two child caregiving time equations. In our case, the model is an endogenous switching tobit model because the caregiving equations also account for the censoring of the observations at zero; that is, one cannot report negative minutes of time devoted to child caregiving. The advantage of this specification is that it models the choice to work any nonstandard hours and allows for the effect of the various regressors used to explain caregiving time to differ by nonstandard work status.

Technically, identification does not require that the determinants of working nonstandard hours and the determinants of caregiving time differ, but in fact, in our specification, state unemployment rates and state women's labor force participation rates are included as determinants of nonstandard work status but not of caregiving hours. In addition, the presence of children enters the determinants of working nonstandard hours differently than as a determinant of caregiving time. When thinking about whether a mother works nonstandard hours, we are interested in whether she has a preschooler versus a school-aged child since the institutional time constraints that preschool and elementary schools represent are quite different. In modeling caregiving time choices, we include a more detailed accounting of the number of children of various ages as determinants of caregiving time just as we do in Chapters 3 and 4.[10]

We have limited our analysis to the caregiving time choices made by mothers who report any hours of paid employment on a weekday diary day. In this way, our study is similar to Wight, Raley, and Bianchi (2008) but differs from Rapoport and Le Bourdais (2008), who model the potential selection into usual employment status directly.[11] While we sidestep the issue of selectivity into employment, our approach permits us to fully account for the potential endogeneity of the nonstandard work choice observed on the diary day. The advantage of our choice is that we are able to discern the differences in the role of demographic, spatial and timing, and economic factors by nonstandard work status.[12]

DETERMINANTS OF WEEKDAY CAREGIVING MINUTES FOR WORKING MOTHERS BY WORK SCHEDULE

Although our primary interest is in the caregiving time equations, Table 5.3 provides the results for the equation that models whether the mother is employed any nonstandard hours on the diary day. What is most striking in Table 5.3 is the lack of many significant predictors of nonstandard work status. Mothers of preschool children are less likely to work any nonstandard hours, while mothers who have another adult in the household (beyond spouses in the case of married mothers) are more likely to work nonstandard hours. A higher predicted price of child care for preschool children also increases the probability of non-standard hours, perhaps because parents work differing schedules to

Table 5.3 Determinants of Working Any Nonstandard Hours on Diary Days

	Probit coefficients
Constant	−2.0973**
Education	0.0050
Age	−0.0046
Husband's earnings if married (thousands)	−0.0285
Married	0.1090
Nonwhite	−0.0531
Hispanic	−0.0942
Urban	−0.0227
South	0.0540
Presence of children aged 0–5	−0.6766***
Presence of children aged 6–12	0.1737
Presence of other adult in household	0.2068**
Summer	0.0574
Predicted ln hourly wages	−0.1932
Predicted price of child care for a 0–5-year-old	0.1411***
Predicted price of child care for a 6–12-year-old	−0.0421
State unemployment rate	−4.0333
State labor force participation rate for women	2.2466***
Predicted usual weekly employment hours	0.0458**

NOTE: **significant at the 0.05 level; ***significant at the 0.01 level.
SOURCE: ATUS 2003–2006.

reduce their expenditure on market child care. Living in a state with a higher women's labor force participation rate increases the probability that a mother works nonstandard hours. Finally, women who are predicted to be employed more hours per week are also more likely to work nonstandard hours. This shows the connection between longer hours and working nonstandard hours.

Table 5.4 presents the marginal effects of the determinants of caregiving hours. Columns (1) and (2) show the determinants of total caregiving minutes for nonstandard and then standard workers. The two columns show somewhat different patterns of significant determinants of total child caregiving time. Other things equal, older mothers who work nonstandard hours devote fewer minutes to caregiving. In contrast, age is not a determinant of the caregiving time of mothers who work only standard hours. As might be expected, mothers with either work schedule devote more minutes to caregiving when there are infants in the household. However, having an additional infant increases the number of minutes of caregiving by 20 minutes for nonstandard workers but by 46 minutes for standard workers. The much larger effect on standard workers mostly is due to their availability in the early morning and in the evening when most caregiving occurs.

Note that the marginal effect of "Summer" (a 0–1 indicator to show the diary day was in June, July, and August) is negative for mothers regardless of their work schedules, but only significant and larger in absolute value for standard working mothers. This is an indication that schoolwork or after-school activities may be the cause of the increased hours of caregiving of standard hours working mothers.

The last set of significant variables in the analysis is the price of time variables: the predicted hourly wage and the predicted price of child care for 0–5-year-olds.[13] Comparing the results across columns (1) and (2), we find that the importance of these price of time variables varies by the mother's work schedule. Mothers with any nonstandard hours with higher wages are statistically significantly likely to spend more minutes in primary caregiving. For working mothers with only standard hours, the wage effect is not significant though the magnitude of the effect is similar.[14] Remember that we find in Chapter 3 a strong positive of the mother's wage on her caregiving hours. Based on the findings in the current chapter, we conclude that the earlier noted result is driven by mothers working any nonstandard hours. For both

Table 5.4 Marginal Effects of Determinants of Weekday Minutes Spent in Caregiving for Mothers with Positive Hours of Employment on That Same Diary Day

	(1) Total child care hours for those with *any* nonstandard employment hours	(2) Total child care hours for those with *no* nonstandard employment hours
Education	−4.2685	−2.6001
Age	−1.2343**	1.0918
Husband's earnings if married (thousands)	−0.0420	1.5052
Married	−1.1932	−12.0524
Nonwhite	−8.9211	−6.3056
Hispanic	−12.3257	−4.6583
Urban	−9.4613	−5.9553
South	−2.2003	32.6583**
No. of children aged 0–2	19.9100*	46.1144*
No. of children aged 3–5	7.9696	2.9754
No. of children aged 6–9	6.4074	13.0855
No. of children aged 10–12	3.6893	6.4221
No. of children aged 13–17	−1.5632	−2.1085
Presence of other adult in household	4.6996	3.3510
Summer	−6.4373	−33.7979***
Predicted ln hourly wage	47.6705*	41.4896
Predicted price of child care for a 0–5-year-old	3.6387**	9.0866***
Predicted price of child care for a 6–12-year-old	0.0588	0.5106
Predicted usual weekly employment hours	2.7832	−7.3597
N	1,093	801

NOTE: *significant at the 0.10 level; **significant at the 0.05 level; ***significant at the 0.01 level.

SOURCE: ATUS 2003–2006.

categories of working mothers, increasing the price of child care for preschool-aged children increases total caregiving minutes, but the magnitude of the effect is larger for mothers working only standard hours. It is likely that the price of preschool child care matters more to standard working mothers because they are more likely to use formal types of child care (Kimmel and Powell 2006a,b).

It is interesting to note that neither the presence of other adults in the household nor the predicted number of employment hours per week has a significant effect on caregiving time for either group of working mothers. Recall that both of these variables were strong predictors of working any nonstandard hours. In other words, the availability of other adults in the household makes it possible for mothers of young children to work nonstandard hours, but it does not affect the number of minutes of caregiving these same mothers devote to their children. Similarly, working more hours per week increases the probability of working non-standard hours but does not directly affect the amount of time mothers spend on caregiving. This is further evidence that mothers shift their own time around to protect their time with children, regardless of the other resources available to them. We saw this also in Chapter 4, when mothers whose husbands spent more time in caregiving activities also spent more time in caregiving activities.[15]

CONSIDERING THE MINUTES OF CAREGIVING IN THE PEAK MORNING AND EVENING TIME SLOTS

Pushing beyond the question of how working nonstandard hours affects total minutes of caregiving, we also can use the time of day information in the ATUS to ask the more specific questions: how do employment hours in the early morning affect mothers' caregiving time in the early morning, and how do employment hours in the evening affect mothers' caregiving time in the evening? We define the early morning period as between 5 a.m. and 8 a.m. Here the indicator variable takes on a value of one if the mother has any paid work time during that early morning period. The measure of caregiving in this case is the caregiving time recorded for that same time period. We would expect that being employed during the early morning period would affect the amount of caregiving that the mother performs during the same period, with the determinants of caregiving differing depending on whether one is employed during that time period. Similarly, we focus on caregiving time in the evening, defined as 6 p.m. to midnight. Here the indicator variable takes on a value of one if the mother is employed during the evening hours and the measure of caregiving time records the caregiving that takes place in those same evening hours.[16]

Table 5.5 shows the determinants of early morning and evening work hours. The two time periods appear to differ conceptually with different factors affecting the choices made at the beginning and the end of the day. For example, having another adult in the household increases the probability of working evening hours but does not affect the probability of working in the early morning. Similarly, having a preschooler reduces the probability of working in the evening but has no effect on the probability of employment hours in the early morning. Conversely, having school-aged children increases the probability of working in the early morning but has no effect on evening hours. Mothers with higher wages and mothers married to men with higher earnings are less likely to work in the evening. Higher child care costs for preschoolers increase the probability of working in the evening but do not affect the probability of working in the morning. Higher child care costs for school-aged children reduce the probability of working early hours but do not affect the probability of working in the evening. As we would expect, mothers who are usually employed more hours per week are more likely to work both morning and evening hours.

Table 5.6 displays the caregiving regression results by work schedule that focus separately on the early morning caregiving time and then the evening caregiving time. Columns (1) and (2) compare the determinants of the amount of early morning caregiving between mothers working some early morning minutes and those working no morning minutes. Similarly, columns (3) and (4) compare the determinants of the amount of evening caregiving between mothers working some time in the evening and those working no evening minutes. Recall though that all mothers in these samples work some minutes for pay on their diary day.

Considering first the demographic variables, the mother's education and age, her husband's earnings, and being married are not significantly associated with the amount of either early morning or evening care-

Table 5.5 Determinants of Working Any Hours in the Early Morning or in the Evening on the Diary Day

	Morning work	Evening work
Constant	−3.9551***	−1.2650
Education	−0.0486	0.1075*
Age	−0.0068	0.0080
Husband's earnings if married (thousands)	−0.0091	−0.0502**
Married	0.1770	−0.0085
Nonwhite	−0.1313	0.0190
Hispanic	−0.1551	−0.0078
Urban	−0.0428	0.0426
South	0.1180	−0.0365
Presence of children aged 0–5	−0.0866	−0.9682***
Presence of children aged 6–16	0.4316***	−0.1025
Presence of other adult in household	0.0292	0.2359**
Summer	−0.0486	0.0580
Predicted ln hourly wages	0.4129	−1.0650*
Predicted price of child care for 0–5-year-olds	0.0089	0.2430***
Predicted price of child care for 6–12-year-olds	−0.0930***	0.0563
State unemployment rate	1.2567	−6.2197
State labor force participation rate for women	2.3416***	1.0404
Predicted usual weekly employment hours	0.0592***	0.0195**

NOTE: Probit coefficients reported. *significant at the 0.10 level; **significant at the 0.05 level; ***significant at the 0.01 level.
SOURCE: ATUS 2003–2006.

giving minutes. Nonwhite mothers with no evening work hours spent less time on caregiving in the evening than white mothers. This pattern is not repeated for morning caregiving time.

The role of children in determining caregiving time varies by the age of the children and the mother's work schedule. For example, for mothers who do not work in the evening, having an infant increases evening caregiving time by approximately 30 minutes, but for mothers

Table 5.6 Marginal Effects of Determinants of Minutes Spent in Morning or Evening Caregiving for Mothers with Positive Hours of Employment during That Same Time Period

	(1) Morning child care hours for those with any morning employment hours	(2) Morning child care hours for those with no morning employment hours	(3) Evening child care hours for those with any evening employment hours	(4) Evening child care hours for those with no evening employment hours
Education	−4.2685	−2.6001	0.2028	3.0691
Age	−1.2343	1.0918	−0.0839	0.4354
Husband's earnings if married (thousands)	−0.0420	1.5052	0.1123	0.7856
Married	−1.1932	−12.0524	−2.1561	−4.6437
Nonwhite	−8.9211	−6.3056	2.4711	−15.9596*
Hispanic	−12.3257	−4.6583	1.9913	−12.8040
Urban	−9.4613	−5.9553	−1.0821	10.7592
South	−2.2003	32.6583	2.8418	−5.1390
No. of children aged 0–2	19.9100	46.1144	−2.3249	27.3485***
No. of children aged 3–5	7.9696	2.9754	−3.9926	9.0250
No. of children aged 6–9	6.4074	13.0855	−1.9840	15.0840**
No. of children aged 10–12	3.6893	6.4221	−0.8992	7.0047*
No. of children aged 13–17	−1.5632	−2.1085	−4.3103***	5.4949
Presence of other adult in household	4.6996*	3.3510	1.9801	0.3744
Summer	−6.4373*	−33.7979***	1.2687	−8.9425***

115

Predicted hourly wage	47.6705	41.4896	5.1452	-12.4209
Predicted price of child care for 0–5-year-old	3.6387*	9.0866**	0.5661	4.4399**
Predicted price of child care for 6–12-year-old	0.0588	0.5106*	-0.1413	-0.0388
Predicted usual weekly employment hours	2.7832	-7.3597	-0.9008	3.0511
N	830	1,064	343	1,551

NOTE: * significant at the 0.10 level; ** significant at the 0.05 level; *** significant at the 0.01 level.
SOURCE: ATUS 2003–2006.

who do work in the evening, there is no increase in caregiving minutes if the child is an infant. Having a young school-aged child also increases evening caregiving time for mothers with no evening work hours by 15 minutes for those with a 6–9-year-old and 7 minutes for those with a 10–12-year-old. For mothers who are employed during the evening hours, there is no effect of having school-aged children on the evening caregiving time. These findings are especially important because that evening time for school-aged children reflects homework time, extra-curricular lessons, and structured bedtimes, all of which are thought to be important for success in school. Wight, Raley, and Bianchi (2008) find that maternal evening work has a negative impact on mothers' involvement with children's education-related activities and time spent reading to children. Note that our category of caregiving is broader, and our model accounts for the potential endogeneity of the choice to work in the evening. However, our findings are consistent with theirs in the sense that mothers of young school-aged children would be expected to spend more evening hours caring for children compared to those with older children, and we see this for standard-hour working mothers but not for mothers who work during the evening on the diary day.

Also of interest is the role of another (nonspouse) adult in the household on mothers' observed caregiving time. One might expect that the availability of additional potential caregivers would reduce maternal caregiving minutes. The opposite is true for those with any morning hours. The presence of the other adult increases the amount of caregiving time mothers with any morning employment hours spend on child caregiving in those same morning hours. It could be that the other adult is doing other tasks that compete with caregiving.

Turning to the importance of the season, recall that Table 5.4 shows that caregiving minutes in the summer are lower for mothers regardless of their work schedules, although the reduction is much larger for mothers working only standard hours. Using Table 5.6, we can see that the large negative effect of summer for standard-hour working mothers is driven equally by reductions in caregiving time in the morning and in the evening. The morning caregiving hours of those mothers working for pay in the morning are also reduced, but by a much smaller amount, and evening caregiving time is not significantly affected by the summer for those mothers working evening hours. One interpretation of these results is that summer reduces the time of day constraints of young children, which reduces the amount of caregiving time of any adult who would have been responding to those time constraints.

Moving on to the economic factors (namely, the wage measure and the two child care price measures), we find that the wage is not a significant determinant of caregiving time use in the morning or in the evening. The price of child care for preschool-aged children is a significantly positive predictor of maternal caregiving for mothers who do not work in the morning or evening hours and for mothers who work nonstandard schedules in the morning. Those working nonstandard schedules in the evening are not affected by higher predicted child care prices. Clearly, mothers working standard hours only are more responsive to higher market child care prices, as they are most likely to use these market services. This positive price response for standard working mothers is also observed in the morning for the price of school-aged children's child care, but not in the evening. Finally, the predicted number of hours employed per week does not impact morning or evening caregiving time on a daily basis.

CONCLUSIONS

The many analyses of mothers' caregiving and employment time presented above have shown that the time that mothers actively care for their children is influenced by their hours of employment, though the trade-off is far from one for one. In fact, the analyses in Chapters 3 and 4 show that employed mothers shield their children from most of the effect of their increased employment hours by cutting back on leisure and home production rather than caregiving.[17] This chapter examines another aspect of employment beyond the total hours spent in employment, that is, the time of day when employment takes place. The timing of paid work across the day is hypothesized to interact with caregiving time due to time of day constraints created by schools and child care providers.[18] The time of day of employment also is expected to affect caregiving time to the extent that another adult is present at home when employment schedules of husbands and wives, for example, do not entirely overlap. Presser (2003) has argued that families sometimes choose nonoverlapping work schedules as a child care strategy.

Our descriptive examination of new U.S. time diary data reveals that employed mothers with children under the age of 13 who work *any* nonstandard hours record 31 fewer minutes of caregiving on the diary day, which is accounted for by 8 fewer minutes in the early morning, 12 fewer minutes during the middle of the day, and 12 fewer minutes in the evening. Certainly, this is not a tremendous difference in total maternal time devoted to caregiving. An examination of hour-by-hour activity shows that most child caregiving occurs in the morning and evening, but that mothers who work nonstandard hours have a distribution of care that is slightly less bimodal than those working standard hours only.

Because working nonstandard hours reflects, in part, family choices, we model the determinants of caregiving time contingent on the nonstandard paid work decision. We estimate three endogenous switching tobit models, looking first at total hours of caregiving, then separately at hours of early morning caregiving and evening caregiving.

Two important results emerge from these analyses. First, the strong positive effect of mothers' predicted wages on caregiving time found in Chapter 3 appears largely to be the result of the strong wage effect for mothers who perform some of their paid work during nonstandard hours. For standard hours–only workers, no such significant wage effect is found, though the coefficient is positive and of similar magnitude.[19] Second, the role of children varies by the age of the child and the mother's work schedule. Having an infant is associated with increased caregiving minutes regardless of work schedule (though the effect is much bigger for standard time workers), but having older school-aged children is associated significantly with increased evening caregiving only for mothers who work exclusively during standard hours. Third, a higher price of preschool care is associated with more maternal caregiving time overall but appears to be especially relevant to mothers working standard hours. This result supports the hypothesis that time constraints for families arise in part from the rigidity of opening and closing times for formal child care.

Notes

1. See also Han (2005) and Grosswald (2004) for discussions of the implications of parental nonstandard work schedules for children and families.
2. Note that work-related travel is included in total work time.
3. Han (2004) also finds that mothers working nonstandard shifts rely heavily on paternal child care for their children. Henly, Ananat, and Danziger (2006) extend Han's work by focusing on low-income mothers. They find that low-income mothers who work in the evening use less center care but more total hours of nonparental care per year.
4. Venn (2004) describes this model as well.
5. In fact, some school systems still switch the child from morning to afternoon kindergarten halfway through the school year.
6. Venn (2004) and Wight, Raley, and Bianchi (2008) also limit their analysis to employed women.
7. Because nonstandard workers are employed more hours on the diary day than standard workers, the effects we observe in this table may be the result of long hours rather than the result of nonstandard hours. In the multivariate analysis, we control for predicted usual weekly employment hours in order to differentiate between the long hour effect and the nonstandard hours effect.
8. These means are unweighted because they reflect estimation sample descriptive statistics.
9. Note that we are speaking here of the work schedule reported on the diary day, not a "usual" work schedule. Rapoport and Le Bourdais (2008) focus on the endogeneity of the usual schedule while treating the schedule reported on the diary day as exogenous.
10. We must also think about identification of the predicted wages, the child care prices, and usual weekly employment hours. The determinants of wages and child care prices include a long list of state contextual variables designed to capture institutional differences in the labor market and the child care market. Additionally, those two instrumenting equations include quadratic terms for age and education and an interaction term between age and education. Usual weekly employment hours are identified by the same quadratic terms for age and education and the interaction term between age and education. The estimation of the usual hours of employment is similar to that in Chapter 4 except that it does not include information about the mother's spouse other than monthly earnings.
11. Rapoport and Le Bourdais's (2008) selection terms (employed or not, and if employed, nonstandard or standard in the usual weekly sense) in their two-stage model are never statistically significant.
12. We did estimate an alternative model in which we use an endogenous switch to estimate caregiving time use simultaneously with total paid work hours (both modeled as tobits) to incorporate the jointness of those two time choices. The coefficient estimates in the caregiving equations were nearly identical.

13. Kimmel and Powell (2006a,b) find substantively different child care price elasticities of modal choices by nonstandard work status, and this varying role of prices may carry over to time uses as well.

14. One reason for the noise in the effect of wages on caregiving hours may be because of the gap in time between the collection of the wage information in the survey (it is collected in the last CPS interview) and the time diary collection. This gap is at least four months.

15. Readers may wonder to what extent our results reported in Tables 5.3 and 5.4 are the result of our more expansive definition of nonstandard work as any minutes of time beyond the (somewhat broadened) hours of 8 a.m. to 6 p.m. We reestimate our full model using the more restrictive categorization of nonstandard work, and this modification has no substantive effect on our results.

16. As the time periods get shorter, the ultimate time constraint would seem to get tighter; that is, if the mother is spending some of this time in employment, then that time is not available for caregiving. But there is still "wiggle room" in the sense that there are many other things she could be doing with her time, such as sleeping, personal care, housework, or leisure.

17. Also see Bianchi (2000) and Howie et al. (2006).

18. Stewart (forthcoming) examines another aspect of the time of day of parental caregiving by considering the time of day of parent-child interactions. He argues that children are most alert around 11 a.m., when most employed parents are not with them.

19. Recall that the analysis in Chapter 3 includes women who were not employed. Their predicted wage may also have significant impacts on maternal caregiving time. Also recall that 58 percent of the women in the "working on a weekday" sample did have some nonstandard hours.

6
Concluding Remarks

Time is our most scarce resource and children our most precious. Raising children, especially young children, is inherently time intensive for parents, especially for mothers, who in every country serve as primary caregivers for most children. We refer to the child-rearing time of mothers as maternal caregiving, and throughout this book we have examined in detail the role that maternal caregiving time plays in U.S. mothers' days.

Caring for children requires trade-offs: spending more time or money on children necessarily implies spending less time and money for other purposes. Are any of these trade-offs systematic? This is one of the fundamental questions of this book. In other words, do time allocation decisions differ between mothers with younger versus older children, higher-wage mothers versus lower-wage mothers, or married mothers versus unmarried mothers? Beyond the characteristics of the mothers themselves and the characteristics of their children, we also explore the role that fathers play in mothers' time trade-offs. Do mothers with husbands who are employed many hours per week make different time choices than mothers whose husbands work fewer hours per week? Does mothers' time with children depend on their husbands' time with children? Finally, we examine whether the time of day when employment occurs has implications for maternal caregiving time and the timing of that caregiving.

We began with a descriptive look at mother's time use and then turned to a statistical examination of the nature of caregiving and the ways that it differs from other time uses. All of our analyses are based on the ATUS, an annual product of the U.S. Census Bureau and the Bureau of Labor Statistics. After nearly 10 years of development, the ATUS was initiated in 2003 and the first data from this annual ongoing survey were released in January of 2005. In Chapter 2, we described this new time diary data source in detail, such as how the data are collected, the sampling, and the way time is categorized. The most important characteristics of the ATUS for our purposes are that sample sizes are large, there is substantial demographic information available in addition to the time diaries, and only one 24-hour time period is recorded with an oversampling of weekend days. In addition, only one time diary is collected per household, although we know much about the demographic characteristics of the other members of the household. In Chapter 2 we also described the choices available in defining maternal caregiving time in the ATUS. While our statistical analyses in later chapters focused on the measure of caregiving that we refer to as primary caregiving, in Chapter 2 we explored two other potential measures: secondary caregiving and "time with children" in order to provide a fuller picture of maternal caregiving.

The ATUS is not an ideal data source for a variety of reasons. First, the 24 hours of time use information is collected by recall rather than by an ongoing time diary in which activities are recorded during the particular 24-hour period. Still, the recall time is only one day instead of a week or a year, as is required in other data surveys. The strategy of a one-day recall has been well tested and judged to be a good trade-off between overly invasive continuous surveys versus a longer recall period. A second concern is that only one day of time diary information is collected, and this single day reflects merely a random snapshot of the respondent's time use. We cannot determine how typical the survey day is for respondents. This is less of a problem when one's research goal is to assess average behavior but becomes highly problematic for seeking individual level causality, such as how the amount of time spent exercising affects a respondent's weight. Our research questions fall somewhere in the middle as we try to predict time use rather than assess the value of that time use for other outcome variables. The third and most important shortcoming of the survey design, from our perspective, is that only a single time diary per household is collected. This is problematic as we are interested in the interplay between mothers' time use and their husbands'. To compensate for this last problem, we develop a statistical methodology to estimate husbands' time use using the time diaries of fathers.

One of the ATUS's many strengths is that time is categorized very precisely. We collapse the more than 300 detailed ATUS time use activities into five broad categories: 1) paid work (including travel to and from work); 2) active leisure (excluding sleep, personal care time, and investment in human capital); 3) caregiving reported as a primary activity; 4) unpaid household work; and 5) a composite "other" category that includes all remaining activities. Chapter 2 provides a descriptive overview of how mothers in the United States use their time in these five categories. Using simple pie charts and bar graphs, we compare the breakdown of time use for various subgroups of mothers based on weekday versus weekend diaries, the age of the youngest child, employment status, and marital status. As is shown in that chapter, mothers of children aged 0–12 spend about 10 percent of their time in caregiving on weekdays and slightly less on weekends. That less time is allocated to caregiving on weekends partially is the result of the definition of primary caregiving (secondary or time with children is higher on weekends) and partially a result of the increased availability of alternative caregivers on weekends.

As expected, mothers of preschoolers devote substantially more of their daily time to primary caregiving (13 percent for these mothers versus 7 percent for mothers of older children). This difference is statistically significant at the 1 percent level. If we include "time with children" in addition to primary caregiving time, the weekday numbers vary from 467 minutes (almost 8 hours) for children aged 0–5 compared to 311 minutes for children 6–12. We also divided primary caregiving into developmental care and other primary care. Developmental care includes time spent talking and playing with children, reading to children and helping with homework, arts and crafts, and homeschooling. Other primary child care activities include mainly the physical care of children, but also time making child care arrangements and travel time related to caregiving. Interestingly, we find the proportion of primary caregiving time that is developmental significantly declines as the child ages. In addition, the proportion is significantly lower on weekends compared to weekdays.

Because time is limited by the 24-hour day, devoting time to caregiving necessarily implies less time available for other time uses. As shown in Chapter 2, the increased caregiving time of mothers of preschoolers is drawn mainly from leisure and paid work because time in household production and other time uses are largely constant across mothers of different aged children. Weekends consistently find mothers doing more home production and less paid employment. They also sleep more on weekends (nice!!) and devote less time to primary caregiving.

Unpaid household work and caregiving represent a substantial portion of a parent's typical weekday: 26 percent of a married mother's day and 10 percent of a married father's day. Clearly, the father's contribution to a family's "output" is nontrivial, implying that upon divorce, a mother faces the potential loss of spousal income as well as spousal family time inputs. Currently, public policy concerning child support does not reflect the divorcee's increased time pressures as well as the increased cost of outsourcing family chores, including caregiving. A more comprehensive view of spousal support would incorporate the lost time as well as lost income associated with the noncustodial parent.

Other interesting observations reported in Chapter 2 concern the differences in time use by marital status and the interaction between caregiving and paid work. On both weekdays and weekends, single mothers devote less time to primary caregiving than married mothers. This difference remains even after we control for the age of their youngest child (using the broad categories of preschoolers, young school-aged children, and teenagers). This suggests a time crunch on the part of single mothers who lack the availability of other adults in the household to contribute to unpaid household production. Note however, that single mothers are more likely to be engaged in paid work and likely to be less educated, both characteristics associated with reduced caregiving. The children of single mothers receive less caregiving time from their mothers and probably less from their fathers as well, such that children of single mothers are disadvantaged in time inputs as well as in income.

There are a number of potential policy reforms that might address the disadvantages faced by children of single mothers. For example, Head Start could be expanded, providing educational and quality caregiving to more children. For school-aged children, after-school care programs could be more readily available and could focus more on academics. This is particularly important for children of single mothers because single mothers are represented disproportionately in the nonstandard work sector, working for pay during the important after-school hours during which homework is completed. Finally, policymakers could revisit welfare policies reformed in the late 1990s to encourage single mothers' employment. If this work time harms children, there may be child welfare arguments in support of relaxing some of these work requirements.

It is clear that some paid work comes at the expense of reduced caregiving, as nonemployed mothers average 200 minutes of caregiving on weekdays while mothers employed full time average 101 minutes. However, the bulk of the time devoted to paid work is drawn from other time uses, not caregiving. Also, somewhat reassuringly, research has shown that, while maternal employment has been on the rise over the course of the past half century, hours devoted to primary caregiving have actually increased (Bryant and Zick 1996; Ramey and Francis 2006; Sayer, Bianchi, and Robinson 2004). Clearly, mothers engaging in paid work have found ways to balance market work with family responsibilities without ignoring childrearing responsibilities.

In Chapter 3, we moved on to a more rigorous analysis of time use by examining the role that economic, demographic, and spatial factors play in mothers' time use decisions. According to Gronau (1977), economic models ought to treat time use categories as distinct if their choices are influenced differentially by these factors. We use multivariate analysis to determine if caregiving is indeed a distinct time choice from other time choices, and more specifically, to determine if caregiving, an unpaid activity, behaves more like unpaid housework or leisure.

Our results show that maternal caregiving behaves in some ways like unpaid housework, and in other ways like leisure, but in many ways caregiving appears distinct from both. Most importantly, we find that caregiving responds positively to an increase in the mother's wage, while both leisure and home production respond in the opposite fashion. In other words, higher-wage mothers devote more time to caregiving, other things equal. This suggests to us that the investment aspect of caregiving is important to these mothers, as mothers devote increased time to caregiving to invest in the future well-being of their children. Ramey and Ramey (2008) argue that as the earnings premium associated with a college education rises in the face of increasingly competitive college admittance, highly educated parents strengthen their focus on child development. Others argue that an increased awareness of crime creates heightened concern for children's safety, but this argument has been rebutted by Ramey and Ramey, who note that crime rates have fallen in recent years. However, there still may be increased concern with child safety, as fewer adults are home in the afternoons when children return from school. With few adults present, having children roam freely throughout their neighborhoods is of greater concern.

This may lead to more scheduled after-school activities, which require greater parental involvement, particularly in transportation.

While college admissions and child safety may help to explain the positive relationship between mothers' wages and caregiving time, we believe that one should imagine the investment component of child caregiving more broadly, as including investments in children's happiness, physical and emotional health, and a lifetime of connectedness and caring between parents and children. Higher-wage mothers may be more willing to invest time in the present in order to receive future returns for their children, just as they have been more willing to invest in their labor market productivity. This finding is also consistent with other research, including that of Guryan, Hurst, and Kearney (2008), who explain that higher-educated mothers devote more time to caregiving for investment purposes.

Alternatively, the increased caregiving associated with higher-wage mothers may simply be the result of the standard income effect—that is, that high-wage mothers have higher incomes and they choose to spend part of that income on their children. These mothers are better able to afford services that reduce home production time, such as dry cleaners, or hiring someone to cook and clean, and they use that saved time to spend more time with their children. The income effect alone, though, does not explain why leisure is reduced for higher-wage mothers. It may be that leisure is the casualty of the substitution effect of more work hours, while home production time is the casualty of increased caregiving time. More research must be done to understand the full implications of our very robust finding that a higher wage is associated with increased caregiving time.

If the positive relationship between maternal wages and primary caregiving time reflects an income effect, then tax policies that increase parental income may generate an equivalent outcome. For example, child subsidies (such as the dependent care tax credit) may lead to increased maternal caregiving time. Blau (2001) has recommended child credits not contingent on maternal employment as a valuable social policy.

Many other demographic factors play their expected roles in mothers' time use decision making, such as marital status. Other things equal, married mothers devote less time to caregiving probably because of the availability of their husbands as care providers. Mothers who are married, other things equal, devote more time to household production and more time to paid work, both likely influenced by the availability of spousal care. These findings show the importance of proceeding beyond the descriptive analyses of Chapter 2, where we showed that, in gross terms, single mothers spend less time on caregiving than married mothers. Some of the confounding factors are hours of employment, and the number of children and their ages. Single mothers have fewer and older children and work more hours in the labor market.

For married mothers, having a husband with higher earnings is associated with significantly more leisure, caregiving, and home production on weekdays and fewer minutes of employment. On weekends, spousal earnings have a much smaller impact, significantly increasing caregiving time a small amount and decreasing employment time. Labor supply research over the last 40 years has found similar significant negative effects of husbands' earnings on women's labor supply, but time diary data allow us to see that the time saved in the labor market is split fairly evenly between the three other uses of time analyzed.

Also of interest in the multivariate analysis findings of Chapter 3 is the role of the structural characteristics of time, particularly the day of the week and the season. Many of the regression findings differed substantially between weekdays and weekends, and in both regressions, the season in which the diary was collected (summer versus not summer) is shown to be an important determinant of time use.[1] This has relevance for real world discussions of time pressures because while some activities are fungible across the week and over the year, other activities, particularly those relating to children, are much less flexible. Differences in weekdays and weekends in the effect of summer diary collection also suggest that the institutional structure of school increases the inflexibility of time for mothers of young school-aged children. Caregiving time in the summer differs less from weekdays to weekend days than it does during the school year.

The results in Chapter 3 also permit us to think about policy questions regarding the role that taxes may play in time use choices. Other things equal, lower taxes imply higher net wages, which our results show lead to more paid work as well as more caregiving. This positive wage effect on paid work has been noted by many other researchers using labor supply surveys such as the CPS. However, producing this result using time diary data might be more convincing, given the short recall time frame and the precision of the work time estimate (both of which result from the particular structure of the ATUS).

Of additional policy concern is the role that child care prices play in time decisions. As shown in Chapter 3, increased child care prices for preschool-aged children lead to increased maternal caregiving. Although the elasticities of child care prices are smaller in magnitude than the corresponding wage elasticities, the child care price elasticities with respect to caregiving are statistically significant for weekday caregiving, implying a role for public policy that alters these prices. Thus, child care subsidies that decrease the price of child care are a mixed bag, facilitating maternal employment during the week but decreasing maternal caregiving. Note that this behavioral response to child care prices is not found for weekends. Additionally, keep in mind that Chapter 4 shows that decreased maternal caregiving associated with increased weekly employment hours is accompanied by increased paternal caregiving, resulting in little net impact on overall child caregiving.

The results in Chapter 3 concerning marital status and husbands' earnings suggest that husbands have an important role in mothers' time choices. To further explore this relationship, in Chapter 4 we discussed a direct examination of husbands' roles in the unpaid time choices of mothers. We considered the effect of relative wages—that is, a mother's wage relative to her husband's in affecting time choices of mothers—as well as husbands' weekly employment hours and husbands' time in an unpaid activity on the mothers' time in the same unpaid activity. The basic multivariate model followed the approach of the previous chapter, with the addition of these three spousal variables.

Predictions about the role of spousal time in mothers' time choices hinge on the fundamental motivation for marriage, that is, the sources of the gains from marriage. If the gains from marriage are due to complementarities, such as enjoying spending leisure time together and performing household tasks together, be they cooking or child raising, then we would predict that an increase in the time in that category of time use of one spouse would increase the time spent in that category of the other spouse. If, however, the mother's gains from marriage result from gains from specialization, where each spouse specializes in tasks at which he or she is relatively better suited, then more time spent in the time category by the husband would mean less time spent by the mother. For example, it takes only one parent to give a young child a bath.

Specialization ignores the utility or disutility of the tasks, focusing only on comparative advantage in production. However, household tasks certainly do differ in the utility or disutility of the task. Noncooperative bargaining models of marriage emphasize relative bargaining power within the household as a determinant of time use patterns.[2] The member of the couple with more relative power should perform fewer of the unpleasant tasks and more of the pleasant tasks. While the effect of relative bargaining power on caregiving is unclear theoretically, given that some tasks involve substantial utility and others considerable disutility, and all involve what we have already characterized as a large investment in the future, the theory does suggest that the higher the relative wage of the mother, the more time she will devote to leisure and the less time she will devote to home production.[3]

In order to confront the problem of having only a single adult time survey per household, we propose a statistical methodology that allows us to construct information for husbands from the information of fathers with time diaries. We refer to this methodology as "out of sample prediction" and explain this procedure in detail in Chapter 4. Recall also, however, that the relative wage variable and the usual weekly hours of employment are available for spouses through the connection between the ATUS and the CPS. Thus, only spouse's time in the same activity is constructed via "out-of-sample prediction."

Overall, our results show little responsiveness in mothers' time choices to spousal factors. This is consistent with Blau and Kahn (2007), who show a declining role of spouses in mothers' paid work choices, and consistent with evidence from Europe showing no effect of husbands' wages on women's caregiving (Hallberg and Klevmarken 2003; Maassen van den Brink and Groot 1997). Specifically, we find no statistically significant role of the relative predicted wage of mothers and their spouses in mothers' time choices for leisure, caregiving, or home production. It could be that money is being traded for time in ways that our time analysis is not capturing or that households are more cooperative than the bargaining models would predict.[4] Alternatively, there are enough household tasks, both pleasant and unpleasant, to go around and, in addition, mothers may trade leisure for caregiving differently than men in ways that are independent of their relative wages.

We find that the husband's usual weekly employment hours are not significant in determining the mother's leisure time, but they do affect her caregiving and household production time choices on weekdays. The husband's usual weekly work hours are positively associated with the mother's caregiving time, while the effect on unpaid housework is negative. This finding is consistent with the fungibility of housework, contrasted with the daily persistence of required caregiving effort.

Perhaps the most interesting finding is the role of husbands' time in the same activity on maternal time choices. Our findings imply that leisure is a complement to husband's leisure on weekdays but a substitute on weekends. In addition, the husband's time in caregiving seems to be complementary to mother's time on weekdays with no effect on weekends. For home production time, the findings are reversed. Home production is shown to be complementary on weekends with no significant effect on weekdays.

In the final empirical chapter of the book, we moved beyond aggregate time measures to examine how the time of day that an activity occurs might matter. In particular, we examined how working outside the traditional daytime hours affects aggregate maternal caregiving as well as maternal caregiving during the crucial before and after school/daycare periods. As is shown in Chapter 2, mothers' primary time with children is distributed bimodally over the course of the day, with peaks in the early morning hours and again in the late afternoon/early evening. We find that mothers who work in the labor market any time outside the 8 a.m. to 6 p.m. time period devote somewhat less time to caregiving overall. We find that higher wages are significantly associated with increased caregiving only for those mothers working any nonstandard hours, although the magnitude of the effect is similar for those working standard hours. This leads to a qualification of the finding in Chapter 3, and implies that mothers working any nonstandard hours may compensate for this paid work occurring "at the wrong time" by investing more hours in total. There is more variation in the behavior of standard time workers in terms of the relationship between wages and total caregiving time, thus the effect of wages on caregiving hours is measured imprecisely. Recall that using the definition of *any* nonstandard hours, more than half of employed mothers fall into the nonstandard category. Also, Chapter 3 includes mothers who are not employed and those employed but not working on the diary day, while Chapter 5 only includes mothers working some minutes on a weekday diary day. Thus, the wage effect in Chapter 3 includes those nonemployed women with higher predicted wages who are also spending more time on caregiving. As such, the two results are not in conflict but offer alternative portraits of the complex issue of wage effects on time use. This finding has policy relevance because the role that parental investment in children plays in their children's future workplace productivity and well-being is substantial.

The price of child care for children aged 0–5 is shown to positively affect the caregiving time of all mothers with some employment hours on their diary day, but the magnitude of the effect is substantially larger for those mothers working only standard hours. Market child care is mostly limited to standard work hours, and thus the price of such care has a greater impact on those mothers whose job hours accommodate the daytime day care hours. Many couples who work nonstandard hours use partners, grandparents, or even the child's siblings as care providers. Some of this relative care is a choice parents have made, while some is the result of the lack of available care (i.e., inadequate supply). A related finding is that the role of family members varies by work schedule and the nature of the family relationship. For example, the presence of another adult in the household (beyond the husband) has a large effect on working nonstandard hours, but not on the amount of caregiving hours for either group of working mothers. Having school-aged children increases the evening caregiving time for those mothers employed standard hours but has no effect on morning caregiving time.

Of course, there is much more analysis one could undertake studying mothers' time choices with the rich data of the ATUS. One important policy area we have only touched on is the full relationship between income and time use. In particular, some researchers have argued that poverty measures should include measures of time as well as money (Douthitt 2000; Vickery 1977). Welfare reform has resulted in more low-income mothers entering the labor market, likely resulting in a reduction in maternal caregiving. But total caregiving time (parental and nonparental combined) for low-income children has probably increased, as mothers have been shown to take time away from other activities in order to provide caregiving time for their children, and the child is cared for in a center or daycare home a substantial part of the day. Whether the children end up better or worse off depends on the quality of nonparental care they receive while the mother is on the job versus the quality of maternal caregiving, and the effects of the time crunch at home.

Of related import is the relationship between time use and maternal well-being. As mothers move into the paid workforce and reduce other time to protect their time with children, maternal well-being may suffer. Thus, policymakers may want to consider parental well-being when formulating welfare, tax, or workplace policy.

High-income mothers also feel substantial time pressure, as they work more hours than low-income mothers and, as we have shown, also spend more time in caregiving. It is not surprising that their fertility rates are lower than low-income women. Still, the time crunch of high-income women is compensated somewhat by the increased likelihood of being married. Their high-income husbands also spend more time in caregiving, leading to what appears to be substantial inequality of time investments between children of high- and low-income families. This time investment gap exacerbates the income gap, perhaps leading to a larger gap in school readiness than researchers had understood previously. If our national education policy is to level the playing field, more investments must be made in low-income children, both in terms of money resources and developmental caregiving time.

Given the time crunch all employed mothers of young children face, government may be able to play a role by promoting policies that facilitate workplace flexibility and an acknowledgment of the difficulties of the dual demands of work and family. One example researched by Connelly, DeGraff, and Willis (2004) is employer-provided child care. They find that most workers (with or without young children) place a high value on on-site child care, likely due in part to the resulting reduction in transportation time, the ease of monitoring such care, and the proximity to children during work hours. Workers without children value that their co-workers miss fewer work hours and are a bit less frazzled. Policymakers can encourage employers to provide this benefit via tax incentives.

Overall, our findings from this research lead to three fundamental conclusions. First, the finding that caregiving is behaviorally distinct from paid work, leisure, and household production should serve as the final death knell to the traditional labor/leisure model of time choice, or even the three-way choice models of employment, leisure, and home production time. Second, our findings show that caregiving plays a complex role in women's lives, yielding difficult trade-offs, both with regard to time choices as well as maternal and child well-being. Some time use appears movable across days of the week or hours of the day, while other tasks require confronting more rigid schedules. The choices of husbands and wives appear somewhat related, though the effects are small and their time appears to be more complementary than substitutable. Third, caregiving is an important economic phenomenon: mothers of young children spend a substantial amount of time each day on caregiving tasks, and this recognition goes beyond narrow policy recommendations. Our nation lacks a cohesive, umbrella child care/early education policy, and discussion needs to move beyond policies that only target maternal employment for low-income women. Caregiving is a huge economic sector, affecting most families and employing many workers, mostly women, many of whom are mothers themselves. Additionally, if national policy were to recognize the inherent value in caregiving, such activity would be incorporated into national income accounts.

As the years of data available from the ATUS grow, increasing sample sizes will allow researchers to look at more narrow categories of time use and more finely tuned demographic groups to expand further our understanding of the way mothers in the United States use their time. We look forward to these future studies with these promising new data and hope that some of the methods developed in this book will be useful for that future research. For as Ralph Waldo Emerson (1837) reminded us, "This time, like all times, is a very good one, if we but know what to do with it."

Notes

1. Distinguishing among the other three seasons did not yield any significant differences.
2. Pollak (2005) argues that relative predicted wages are the best measure of relative bargaining power. This is the measure we use in our analysis.
3. This same prediction is generated by equilibrium marriage models such as Becker (1973) and Grossbard-Shechtman (1984, 2003).
4. Grossbard-Shechtman (2003) argues for a model of marriage and work in the household in which husbands and wives directly trade time in household production for access to money within the marriage.

Appendix A
ATUS Time Use Categories Included in Five Aggregate Time Uses

Table A.1 Time Use Categories Included in Five Aggregate Time Uses

Leisure	100200-100299	Civic obligations and participation
	110100-119999	Eating and drinking
	120100-129999	Socializing, relaxing, and leisure
	130100-139999	Sports, exercise, and recreation
	140100-149999	Religious and spiritual activities
	150100-159999	Volunteer activities
	160100-160102	Telephone calls to/from friends and family
	170401-170488	Travel related to caring for and helping nonhousehold members
	171004	Travel related to civic obligations and participation
	171100-179999	Travel related to eating and drinking
Caregiving	030100-030399	Caring for and helping household children, activities related to children's education and health
	080100-080199	Child care services
	170301	Travel related to caring for and helping household children
	170801	Travel related to using child care services
Home production	020000-029999	Household activities
	030400-039999	Caring for and helping household adults and members
	040000-049999	Caring for and helping nonhousehold members (adults and children)
	080200-080399	Financial services, banking, and legal services
	080600-089999	Real estate, veterinary services, security procedures, and other professional/personal services
	090000-099999	Household services
	100100-100199	Using government services
	100300-109999	Waiting associated with, and security procedures related to, government services/civic obligations
	160104-169999	Telephone calls to/from salespeople, profes./Pers./Household service providers, paid adult or child care providers and government officials

	170200-170299	Travel related to household activities
	170302-170399	Travel related to caring for and helping household members
	170700-170799	Travel related to consumer purchases
	170802-170803	Travel related to using professional and personal care services
	170806-171003	Travel related to using professional and personal care services, household services, and using government services and civic obligations
	171099	Travel related to government services and civic obligations
Employment	050100-050199	Working
	050300-050399	Other income-generating activities
Other	010000-019999	Personal care
	050200-050299	Work-related activities
	050400-050499	Job search and interviewing
	060100-069999	Education time
	080400-080599	Medical and care services, personal care services
	160103	Telephone calls to/from education services providers
	170100-170199	Travel related to personal care
	170500-170699	Travel related to work, education
	170804-170805	Travel related to using medical services and personal care services

Appendix B
The Categorization of Time as Child Caregiving According to the ATUS Survey Coding Rules

Child care: Determining when an activity should be coded as child care (0301xx, 0302xx, or 0303xx) can be difficult. Neither the presence of a child during the respondent's activity nor a child's participation in the respondent's activity is sufficient alone to code the activity as child care:

- Watching cartoons with my child = watching television. (Respondent can watch television—even cartoons!—without the child.)

- Shopping for school clothes with Susie = shopping. (Respondent can shop for Susie's school clothes without the child.)

- Watching the *Lion King* play with my son = arts and entertainment. (Respondent can go to the play without the child.)

- Playing Monopoly with wife and daughter = relaxing/playing games. (Respondent can still play Monopoly with wife if child isn't playing.)

- Talking to my neighbor and her children = socializing and communicating with others. (Respondent can talk even if children are not there.)

When the respondent is directly watching or interacting with a child only, or accompanying a child to an activity that has no purpose outside the child, then code as child care:

- Playing Monopoly with my kids = child care. (Respondent can't play if children are not playing.)

- Keeping an eye on my child = child care. (Without the child, this activity wouldn't even be mentioned.)

- Attending my son's Boy Scout function = child care. (It is the child's activity; without the child, respondent has no purpose in attending function.)

Appendix C
Methods Used to Construct
Price of Time Variables

The three price of time variables are predicted values obtained from initial stage estimation (see Kimmel and Connelly [2007] for further details). We use state economic and policy variables to assist in the identification of the predicted child care expenditure. The predicted wage is obtained, as is typical, by estimating a sample-selection corrected wage equation using ATUS data. We estimate the probability of being in the labor force using a probit model and then estimate log wages correcting for the selection into the labor market.

We would have liked to generate the price of nonparental child care the same way, but the ATUS data do not include child care expenditure information. Instead, to estimate child care costs we used data from the fourth wave of the 2001 Panel of the Survey of Income and Program Participation, which was administered between September and December 2002. Employed women with children under the age of 5 were asked about their expenditures on child care for their youngest child. In addition, employed women with children between the ages of 6 and 14 were asked about their expenditure on child care for their youngest child in that age range. We eliminated those whose youngest child was 13 or 14 and those who were either currently in the military, in school, or unemployed. We used the resulting sample to estimate the price of child care for children age 5 or under and separately for children between the ages of 6 and 12. The procedure we used to estimate the hourly price of child care is a standard bivariate selection correction model which is described by Tunali (1986) and used by Connelly and Kimmel (2003a,b). Using this procedure, we predicted the weekly expenditure on child care, correcting for the self-selection of both being employed and paying for care using the SIPP data. We then use the resulting coefficients and the values of the determinants from the mothers in the ATUS sample to construct the two predicted child care expenditure variables for each mother.

Table C.1 Variable Means of Model Variables, ATUS 2003–2006

	Weekday		Weekend	
	Mean	Standard deviation	Mean	Standard deviation
Independent variables				
Education	13.708	2.927	13.537	3.116
Age	35.017	7.513	35.026	7.333
Husband's earnings if married ($,000)	2.817	2.948	2.806	2.957
Married spouse present	0.661	0.473	0.670	0.470
Nonwhite	0.178	0.383	0.181	0.385
Hispanic	0.163	0.370	0.189	0.392
Urban	0.750	0.433	0.744	0.436
South	0.344	0.475	0.344	0.475
Number of children aged 0–2	0.360	0.563	0.366	0.567
Number of children aged 3–5	0.383	0.578	0.389	0.565
Number of children aged 6–9	0.546	0.664	0.564	0.674
Number of children aged 10–12	0.417	0.574	0.418	0.587
Number of children aged 13–17	0.254	0.521	0.253	0.527
Presence of other adults in the household	0.145	0.352	0.134	0.341
Summer	0.255	0.436	0.250	0.433
Predicted natural log of hourly wage	2.372	0.390	2.353	0.412
Predicted price of child care for child 0–5	2.905	2.778	2.989	2.783
Predicted price of child care for child 6–12	2.047	1.890	2.020	1.922
Dependent variables				
Minutes of leisure time	150.8	134.2	99.5	124.5
Minutes of child caregiving time	222.6	240.5	53.4	149.2
Minutes of home production time	204.4	162.9	256.3	173.7
Minutes of paid employment time	277.5	159.5	406.7	193.1
Number of observations	3,691		4,136	

NOTE: Variable means are unweighted so that they exactly match the multivariate sample. The predicted prices of child care and predicted log hourly wages are derived from preliminary regression analysis. Predicted price of child care is set to zero for mothers with no child in the relevant range.

Appendix D
Theoretical Model
Used in Chapter 4

Maximize individual utility, $U(t_{mL}, t_{fL}, CS, G)$

Subject to:
Household production function: $G = G(t_{mhp}, t_{fhp}, X; \theta)$
Child Services production function: $CS = CS(t_{mcc}, t_{fcc}, t_{cc}, CX; \phi)$
Money budget constraint: $P_X X + P_{cc}t_{cc} + P_{CX}CX = w_m t_{mem} + w_f t_{fem} + V$
Mother's time constraint: $T = t_{mem} + t_{mhp} + t_{mcc} + t_{mL} + t_{ms}$
Husband's time constraint: $T = t_{fem} + t_{fhp} + t_{fcc} + t_{fL} + t_{fs}$
Child time constraint: $CT = t_{mcc} + t_{fcc} + t_{cc} + t_{scc}$

G denotes adult consumption goods.
CS denotes child services.
T is total adult time while CT is total child time.
t_{iL} is leisure, ti_{hp} is home production time, and t_{icc} is caregiving time of the parent, t_{iem} is time in employment, and t_{is} is time in all other time uses (mainly sleep and personal care but also time in human capital investments and unpaid work-related activities) for $i = m$ or f where m denotes mother and f denotes father.

t_{cc} is paid nonparental child care time (purchased at price P_{cc}) and t_{scc} is secondary child caregiving time (time when the parent is engaged in another primary time use activity but is also watching the child).

X is purchased goods which are inputs in the production of adult consumption goods.
θ is an efficiency parameter for the production of adult consumption goods.
P_X is the price of X goods.

CX is purchased goods that are inputs in the production of child services.
ϕ is an efficiency parameter for the production of child services.
P_{CX} is the price of CX goods.

w_i is the hourly wage of each parent.
V is nonearned income.

Note that often in models involving paid child care $t_{cc} = t_{mem}$ but that is not the case here. However, some adult must be with the child at all times unless self care is included in secondary child care.

The model results in mother's time use demand equations that depend on the price of her time, the price of the husband's time, and the spouse's time use in the same activity.

$$t_j = f(E_m, E_f | D, S) \text{ for } j = hp, cc, L$$

E_m denotes economic factors of the mother.
E_f denotes economic factors of her husband (i.e., the father).
D denotes demographic factors.
S denotes time/spatial factors.

References

Abraham, Katharine G., Aaron Maitland, and Suzanne M. Bianchi. 2006. "Nonresponse in the American Time Use Survey: Who Is Missing from the Data and How Much Does It Matter?" *Public Opinion Quarterly* 70(5): 676–703.

Abraham, Katherine, Sara Helms, and Stanley Presser. 2009. "How Social Processes Distort Measurement: The Impact of Survey Nonresponse on Estimates of Volunteer Work in the United States." *American Journal of Sociology* 114(4): 1129–1165.

Aguiar, Mark, and Erik Hurst. 2007. "Measuring Trends in Leisure: The Allocation of Time over Five Decades." *Quarterly Journal of Economics* 122(2): 969–1006.

———. 2008. "The Increase in Leisure Inequality." NBER Working Paper No. 13837. Cambridge, MA: National Bureau of Economic Research.

Allard, Mary, Suzanne M. Bianchi, Jay Stewart, and Vanessa Wight. 2007. "Comparing Childcare Measures in the ATUS and Earlier Time-Diary Studies." *Monthly Labor Review* 130(5): 27–36.

Alvarez, Begona, and Daniel Miles. 2003. "Gender Effect on Housework Allocation: Evidence from Spanish Two-Earner Couples." *Journal of Population Economics* 16(2): 227–242.

Apps, Patricia. 2005. "Gender, Time Use and Public Policy over the Life Cycle." *Oxford Review of Economic Policy* 21(3): 439–461.

Becker, Gary. 1965. "A Theory of the Allocation of Time." *Economic Journal* 75(299): 493–515.

———. 1973. "A Theory of Marriage: Part I." *Journal of Political Economy* 81(4): 813–846.

———. 1991. *A Treatise on the Family*. Boston: Harvard University Press.

Beers, Thomas M. 2000. "Flexible Schedules and Shift Work: Replacing the '9-to-5' Workday?" *Monthly Labor Review* 123(6): 33–40.

Bianchi, Suzanne M. 2000. "Maternal Employment and Time with Children: Dramatic Change or Surprising Continuity?" *Demography* 37(4): 401–414.

Bianchi, Suzanne M., Lynn Casper, and Roselind King, eds. 2005. *Work, Family, Health and Well-Being*. New York: Laurence Erlbaum Associates.

Bianchi, Suzanne M., Melissa A. Milkie, Liana C. Sayer, and John P. Robinson. 2000. "Is Anyone Doing the Housework? Trends in the Gender Division of Household Labor." *Social Forces* 79(1): 191–228.

Bianchi, Suzanne M., John P. Robinson, and Melissa A. Milkie. 2006. *Changing Rhythms of American Family Life*. New York: Russell Sage Foundation.

Bianchi, Suzanne M., Vanessa Wight, and Sara Raley. 2005. "Maternal Employment and Family Caregiving: Rethinking Time with Children in the

ATUS." Paper presented at the "ATUS Early Results Conference," held in Bethesda, MD, December 8–9.

Bittman, Michael, Paula England, Liana Sayer, Nancy Folbre, and George Matherson. 2003. "When Does Gender Trump Money? Bargaining and Time in Household Work." *American Journal of Sociology* 109(1): 186–214.

Bittman, Michael, and Judy Wajcman. 2004. "The Rush Hour: The Quality of Leisure-time and Gender Equity." In *Family Time: The Social Organization of Care*, Nancy Folbre and Michael Bittman, eds. London: Routledge, pp. 171–194.

Blau, David M. 2001. *The Child Care Problem: An Economic Analysis*. New York: Russell Sage Foundation Publications.

Blau, Francine, and Laurence Kahn. 2007. "Changes in the Labor Supply Behavior of Married Women: 1980–2000." *Journal of Labor Economics* 25(3): 393–438.

Blundell, Richard, and Thomas McCurdy. 1999. "Labor Supply: A Review of Alternative Approaches." In *Handbook for Labor Economics*, Vol. 3A. Orley Ashenfelter and David Card, eds. Amsterdam: Elsevier Science, pp. 1559–1695.

Browning, Martin, and Pierre-Andre Chiappori. 1998. "Efficient Intra-household Allocations: A General Characterization and Empirical Tests." *Econometrica* 66(5): 1241–1278.

Bryant, W. Keith, and Cathleen Zick. 1996. "Are We Investing Less in the Next Generation? Historical Trends in Time Spent Caring for Children." *Journal of Family and Economic Issues* 17(3–4): 365–392.

Burda, Michael, Daniel S. Hamermesh, and Philippe Weil. 2007. "Total Work, Gender and Social Norms." Unpublished manuscript; previous draft circulated as IZA Discussion Paper No. 2705. Bonn, Germany: IZA.

Bureau of Labor Statistics (BLS). 2005. "Workers on Flexible and Shift Schedules in May 2004." News release 05-1198. Washington, DC: Department of Labor, Bureau of Labor Statistics, July 1. http://www.bls.gov/news.release/pdf/flex.pdf (accessed April 20, 2010).

———. 2008a. *American Time Use Survey Coding Rules 2007*. Washington, DC: U.S. Department of Labor, BLS.

———. 2008b. *American Time Use Survey User's Guide: Understanding ATUS 2003 to 2007*. Washington, DC: U.S. Department of Labor, BLS. http://www.bls.gov/tus/atususersguide.pdf (accessed July 10, 2010).

Capizzano, Jeffrey, Kathryn Tout, and Gina Adams. 2000. "Child Care Patterns of School-Age Children with Employed Mothers." Occasional Paper No. 41. Washington, DC: Urban Institute. http://www.urban.org/url.cfm?ID=310283 (accessed April 14, 2010).

Casper, Lynne M., and Martin O'Connell. 1998. "Work, Income, the Economy, and Married Fathers as Child-Care Providers." *Demography* 35(2): 243–250.

Casper, Lynne M., and Kristin E. Smith. 2004. "Self-Care: Why Do Parents Leave Their Children Unsupervised?" *Demography* 41(2): 285–301.

Chiappori, Pierre-Andre. 1988. "Rational Household Labor Supply." *Econometrica* 56(1): 63–90.

Chiappori, Pierre-Andre, Bernard Fortin, and Guy Lacroix. 2002. "Marriage Market, Divorce Legislation and Household Labor Supply." *Journal of Political Economy* 110(1): 37–72.

Collins, Ann, Jean I. Layzer, J. Lee Kreader, Alan Werner, and Fred B. Glantz. 2000. *National Study of Child Care for Low-Income Families. State and Community Substudy Interim Report.* Washington, DC: Abt Associates. http://eric.ed.gov/ERICDocs/data/ericdocs2sql/content_storage_01/0000019b/80/16/b3/3a.pdf (accessed April 14, 2010).

Connelly, Rachel. 1992. "The Effect of Child Care Costs on Married Women's Labor Force Participation," *Review of Economics and Statistics* 74(1): 83–90.

Connelly, Rachel, Deborah S. DeGraff, and Rachel A. Willis. 2004. *Kids at Work: The Value of Employer-Sponsored On-Site Child Care.* Kalamazoo, MI: W.E. Upjohn Institute for Employment Research.

Connelly, Rachel, and Jean Kimmel. 2003a. "The Effect of Child Care Costs on Employment and Welfare Recipiency of Single Mothers." *Southern Economic Journal* 69(3): 498–519.

———. 2003b. "Marital Status and Full-time/Part-time Work Status in Child Care Choices." *Applied Economics* 35(7): 761–777.

———. 2008. "Spousal Economic Factors in ATUS Parents' Time Choices." *Social Indicators Research* 93(1): 147–152.

———. 2009a. "Can the Single Diary per Household Problem Be Overcome?" Presented at the American Time Use Research Conference and Workshop, University of Maryland, College Park, June 25–26.

———. 2009b. "Spousal Influences on Parents' Non-Market Time Choices." *Review of Economics of the Household* 7(4): 361–394.

———. Forthcoming. "The Role of Nonstandard Work Status in Parental Caregiving for Young Children." *Eastern Economic Review.*

Craig, Lyn. 2006. "Children and the Revolution: A Time-Diary Analysis of the Impact of Motherhood on Daily Workload." *Journal of Sociology* 42(2): 125–143.

———. 2007. "How Employed Mothers in Australia Find Time for Both Market Work and Childcare." *Journal of Family and Economic Issues* 28(1): 69–87.

Devereux, Paul. 2004. "Changes in Relative Wages and Family Labor Supply." *Journal of Human Resources* 39(3): 696–722.

Douthitt, Robin A. 2000. "Time to Do the Chores? Factoring Home-Production Needs into Measures of Poverty." *Journal of Family and Economic Issues* 21(1): 7–17.

Emerson, Ralph Waldo. 1837. "The American Scholar." Oration delivered before the Phi Beta Kappa Society, Cambridge, MA, August 31.

Fisher, Kimberly. 2005. "Comments on 'Maternal Employment and Family Caregiving: Rethinking Time with Children in the ATUS.'" Presented at the "ATUS Early Results Conference," held in Bethesda, MD, December 8–9.

Fisher, Kimberly, Muriel Egerton, Jonathan Gershuny, and John Robinson. 2006. "Gender Convergence in the American Heritage Time Use Study." ISER Working Paper No. 2006-25. Anchorage, AK: Institute for Social and Economic Research.

Folbre, Nancy, Jayoung Yoon, Kade Finnoff, and Allison Sidle Fuligni. 2005. "By What Measure? Family Time Devoted to Children in the United States." *Demography* 42(2): 373–390.

Fortin, Bernard, and Guy Lacroix. 1997. "A Test of the Unitary and Collective Models of Household Labour Supply." *Economic Journal* 107(443): 933–955.

Fortson, Kenneth N. 2004. "The Diurnal Pattern of On-the-Job Injuries." *Monthly Labor Review* 127(9): 18–25.

Frazis, Harley, and Jay Stewart. 2004. "What Can Time-Use Data Tell Us about Hours of Work?" *Monthly Labor Review* 127(12): 3–9.

Friedberg, Leora, and Anthony Webb. 2006. "The Chore Wars: Household Bargaining and Leisure Time." Unpublished manuscript. University of Virginia, Charlottesville. http://www.virginia.edu/economics/Workshops/papers/friedberg/chore%20wars%208-30-06.pdf (accessed April 14, 2010).

Goldscheider, Frances K., and Linda J. Waite. 1991. *New Families, No Families?* Los Angeles: University of California Press.

Graham, John, and Carole Green. 1984. "Estimating the Parameters of a Household Production Function with Joint Products." *Review of Economics and Statistics* 66(2): 277–283.

Gronau, Reuben. 1977. "Leisure, Home Production and Work: The Theory of the Allocation of Time Revisited." *Journal of Political Economy* 85(6): 1099–1124.

Gronau, Reuben, and Daniel Hamermesh. 2006. "Time vs. Goods: The Value of Measuring Household Production Technologies." *Review of Income and Wealth* 52(1): 1–16.

Grossbard-Shechtman, Shoshana. 1984. "A Theory of Allocation of Time in Markets for Labour and Marriage." *Economic Journal* 94(376): 863–882.

———. 2003. "A Consumer Theory with Competitive Markets for Work in Marriage." *The Journal of Socio-Economics* 31(6): 609–645.

Grosswald, Blanche. 2004. "The Effects of Shift Work on Family Satisfaction." *Families in Society* 85(3): 413–423.

Guryan, Jonathan, Erik Hurst, and Melissa S. Kearney. 2008. "Parental Education and Parental Time with Children." *Journal of Economic Perspectives* 22(3): 23–46.

Hallberg, Daniel. 2003. "Synchronous Leisure, Jointness, and Household Labor Supply." *Labour Economics* 10(2): 185–203.

Hallberg, Daniel, and Anders Klevmarken. 2003. "Time for Children: A Study of Parents' Time Allocation." *Journal of Population Economics* 16(2): 205–226.

Hamermesh, Daniel. 1996. *Workdays, Workhours, Work Schedules: Evidence for the United States and Germany*. Kalamazoo, MI: W.E. Upjohn Institute for Employment Research.

———. 1999. "The Timing of Work over Time." *Economic Journal* 109(452): 37–66.

———. 2002. "Timing, Togetherness and Time Windfalls." *Journal of Population Economics* 15(4): 601–623.

———. 2007. "Time to Eat: Household Production under Increasing Income Inequality." *American Journal of Agricultural Economics* 89(4): 852–863.

Hamermesh, Daniel, Harley Frazis, and Jay Stewart. 2005. "Data Watch: The American Time Use Survey." *Journal of Economic Perspectives* 19(1): 221–232.

Hamermesh, Daniel, and Jungmin Lee. 2007. "Stressed Out on Four Continents: Time Crunch or Yuppie Kvetch?" *Review of Economics and Statistics* 89(2): 374–383.

Hamermesh, Daniel, and Gerard A. Pfann. 2005. "Time-Use Data in Economics." *European Economic Review* 49(1): 1–7.

Han, Wen-Jui. 2004. "Nonstandard Work Schedules and Child Care Decisions: Evidence from the NICHD Study of Early Child Care." *Early Childhood Research Quarterly* 19(2): 231–256.

———. 2005. "Maternal Nonstandard Work Schedules and Child Cognitive Outcomes." *Child Development* 76(1): 137–154.

Hausman, Jerry, and Paul Ruud. 1984. "Family Labor Supply with Taxes." *American Economic Review* 74(2): 242–248.

Heckman, James J. 1979. "Sample Selection Bias as a Specification Error." *Econometrica* 47(1): 153–161.

Hedges, Janice Neipert, and Edward S. Sekscenski. 1979. "Workers on Late Shifts in a Changing Economy." *Monthly Labor Review* 102(9): 14–22.

Henly, Julia R., Elizabeth O. Ananat, and Sandra K. Danziger. 2006. "Nonstandard Work Schedules, Child Care Subsidies, and Child Care Arrangements." Unpublished manuscript, University of Chicago.

Hersch, Joni. 2003. "Wages, Time Use, and Household Decision Mak-

ing." IZA Discussion Paper No. 2894. Bonn, Germany: IZA. http://www
.fundacionareces.es/PDF/hersch.pdf (accessed March 5, 2005).

Hersch, Joni, and Leslie Stratton. 1994. "Housework, Wages and the Division
of Housework Time for Employed Spouses." *American Economic Review*
84(2): 120–125.

———. 2002. "Housework and Wages." *Journal of Human Resources* 37(1):
217–229.

Hill, C. Russell, and Frank Stafford. 1974. "Allocation of Time to Preschool
Children and Educational Opportunity." *Journal of Human Resources* 9(3):
323–341.

Horrigan, Michael, and Diane Herz. 2004. "Planning, Designing, and Execut-
ing the BLS American Time-Use Survey." *Monthly Labor Review* 127(10):
3–19.

Howie, Peter, John Wicks, John M. Fitzgerald, Douglas Dalenberg, and Rachel
Connelly. 2006. "Mothers' Time Spent in Care of Her Children and Market
Work: A Simultaneous Model with Attitudes as Instruments." *Applied Eco-
nomic Letters* 13(8): 503–506.

Jacobsen, Joyce, and Peter Kooreman. 2005. "Timing Constraints and the Allocation of Time: The Effects of Changes in Shopping Hours Regulation in
the Netherlands." *European Economic Review* 49(1): 9–27.

Jenkins, Stephen, and Lars Osberg. 2005. "Nobody to Play With? The Implications of Leisure Coordination." In *The Economics of Time Use*, Daniel
Hamermesh and Gerard Pfann, eds. Amsterdam: Elsevier, pp. 113–145.

Joyce, Mary, and Jay Stewart. 1999. "What Can We Learn from Time-Use
Data?" *Monthly Labor Review* 122(8): 3–6.

Kalenkoski, Charlene, and Gigi Foster. 2008. "The Quality of Time Spent with
Children in Australian Households." *Review of Economics of the Household*
6(3): 243–266.

Kalenkoski, Charlene, David Ribar, and Leslie Stratton. 2005. "Parental Child
Care in Single Parent, Cohabiting, and Married Couple Families: Time
Diary Evidence from the United Kingdom." *American Economic Review*
95(2): 194–198.

———. 2007. "The Effect of Family Structure on Parents' Child Care Time
in the United States and the United Kingdom." *Review of Economics of the
Household* 5(4): 353–384.

Kaufman, Bruce E., and Julie L. Hotchkiss. 2003. *The Economics of Labor Markets*, 6th ed. Toronto: South-Western Press.

Kendig, Sarah M., and Suzanne M. Bianchi. 2008. "Single, Cohabiting, and
Married Mothers' Time with Children." *Journal of Marriage and the Family*
70(5): 1228–1240.

Kim, Jongsoong, and Lydia Zepeda. 2004. "When the Work Is Never Done:

Time Allocation in U.S. Family Farm Households." *Feminist Economics* 10(1): 115–139.

Kimmel, Jean, and Rachel Connelly. 2007. "Mothers' Time Choices: Caregiving, Leisure, Home Production, and Paid Work." *Journal of Human Resources* 42(3): 643–681.

Kimmel, Jean, and Lisa Powell. 2006a. "Nonstandard Work and Child Care Choices of Married Mothers." *Eastern Economic Journal* 32(3): 397–419.

———. 2006b. "Nonstandard Work and Child Care Choices: Implications for Welfare Reform." In *From Welfare to Child Care: What Happens to Young Children When Mothers Exchange Welfare for Work,* Natasha Cabrera, Robert Hutchens, and H. Elizabeth Peters, eds. Mahwah, NJ: Lawrence Erlbaum Associates, Inc., pp. 129–148.

Klevmarken, N. Anders. 2004. "On the Wealth Dynamics of Swedish Families, 1984–98." *Review of Income and Wealth* 50(4): 469–491.

Kooreman, Peter, and Arie Kapteyn. 1987. "A Disaggregated Analysis of the Allocation of Time within the Household." *The Journal of Political Economy* 95(2): 223–249.

Lam, David. 1988. "Marriage Markets and Assortative Mating with Household Public Goods." *Journal of Human Resources* 23(3): 462–487.

Lamb, Michael, Joseph Pleck, and Eric Charnov. 1985. "Parental Behavior in Humans." *American Zoologist* 25: 883–894.

Lundberg, Shelly. 1988. "Labor Supply of Husbands and Wives: A Simultaneous Equations Approach." *Review of Economics and Statistics* 70(2): 224–235.

Lundberg, Shelly, and Robert Pollak. 1993. "Separate Spheres Bargaining and the Marriage Market." *Journal of Political Economy* 101(6): 988–1010.

———. 2007. "The American Family and Family Economics." *Journal of Economic Perspectives* 21(3): 3–26.

Lundberg, Shelly, Robert Pollak, and Terence Wales. 1997. "Do Husbands and Wives Pool Resources: Evidence from the UK Child Benefit." *Journal of Human Resources* 32(3): 463–480.

Maassen van den Brink, Henriette, and Wim Groot. 1997. "A Household Production Model of Paid Labor, Household Work and Child Care." *De Economist* 145(3): 325–343.

Manser, Marilyn, and Murray Brown. 1980. "Marriage and Household Decision Making: a Bargaining Analysis." *International Economic Review* 20(3): 31–44.

McElroy, Marjorie, and Mary Horney. 1981. "Nash-Bargained Decisions: Toward a Generalization of the Theory of Demand." *International Economic Review* 22(2): 333–349.

Mroz, Thomas. 1987. "The Sensitivity of an Empirical Model of Married Women's

Hours of Work to Economic and Statistical Assumptions." *Econometrica* 55(4): 765–799.

National Center for Education Statistics (NCES). 2004. *Digest of Education Statistics*, Table 4. Washington, DC: NCES. http://165.224.221.98/programs/digest/d04/tables/dt04_045.asp/.

National Institute of Child Health and Human Development Early Child Care Research Network. 1994. "Child Care and Child Development: The NICHD Study of Early Child Care." In *Development Follow-ups: Concepts, Domains and Methods*, S.L. Friedman and H.C. Haywood, eds. New York: Academic Press, pp. 377–396.

Nock, Steven, and Paul Kingston. 1988. "Time with Children: The Impact of Couples' Work-Time Commitment." *Social Forces* 67(1): 59–85.

Overturf Johnson, Julia. 2005. "Who's Minding the Kids? Child Care Arrangements: Winter 2002." Current Population Reports P74-101. Washington, DC: U.S. Census Bureau.

Polivka, Anne. 2008. "Day, Evening, and Night Workers: A Comparison of What They Do in Their Nonwork Hours and with Whom They Interact." In *How Do We Spend Our Time,* Jean Kimmel, ed. Kalamazoo, MI: W.E. Upjohn Institute for Employment Research, pp. 141–175.

Pollak, Robert. 2005. "Bargaining Power in Marriage: Earnings, Wage Rates and Household Production." NBER Working Paper No. 11239. Cambridge, MA: National Bureau of Economic Research.

Presser, Harriet B. 1988. "Shift Work and Child Care among Young Dual-Earner American Parents." *Journal of Marriage and the Family* 50(1): 133–148.

———. 2003. *Working in a 24/7 Economy*. New York: Russell Sage Foundation.

———. 2004. "The Economy That Never Sleeps." *Contexts* 3(2): 1–5.

Ramey, Garey, and Valerie Ramey. 2008. "The Rugrat Race." Working paper. University of California, San Diego.

Ramey, Valerie A. 2008. "Time Spent in Home Production in the 20th Century: New Estimates from Old Data." NBER Working Paper No. 13985. Cambridge, MA: National Bureau of Economic Research.

Ramey, Valerie, and Neville Francis. 2006. "A Century of Work and Leisure." NBER Working Paper No. 12264. Cambridge, MA: National Bureau of Economic Research.

Ransom, Michael R. 1987. "An Empirical Model of Discrete and Continuous Choice in Family Labor Supply." *Review of Economics and Statistics* 69(3): 465–472.

Rapoport, Benoit, and Celine Le Bourdais. 2008. "Parental Time and Working Schedules." *Journal of Population Economics* 21(4): 903–932.

Reimer, Cordelia. 2002. "Parents' Work Time and the Family." In *The Economics of Work and Family*, Jean Kimmel and Emily Hoffman, eds. Kalamazoo, MI: W.E. Upjohn Institute for Employment Research, pp. 71–104.

Robbins, Lionel. 1930. "On the Elasticity of Demand for Income in Terms of Efforts." *Economica* 29: 123–129.

Robinson, John, and Geoffrey Godbey. 1997. *Time for Life*. University Park, PA: Pennsylvania State University Press.

Robinson, John, and Ann Bostrom. 1994. "The Overestimated Workweek? What Time Diary Measures Suggest." *Monthly Labor Review* 117(8): 11–23.

Sandberg, John, and Sandra Hofferth. 2001. "Changes in Children's Time with Parents: United States, 1981–1997." *Demography* 38(3): 423–436.

———. 2005. "Changes in Children's Time with Parents: A Correction." *Demography* 42(2): 391–395.

Sayer, Liana. 2005. "Gender, Time and Inequality: Trends in Women's and Men's Paid Work, Unpaid Work and Free Time." *Social Forces* 84(1): 285–303.

Sayer, Liana, Suzanne M. Bianchi, and John Robinson. 2004. "Are Parents Investing Less in Children? Trends in Mothers' and Fathers' Time with Children." *American Journal of Sociology* 110(1): 1–43.

Smeeding, Timothy, and Joseph T. Marchand. 2004. "Family Time and Public Policy in the United States." In *Family Time: The Social Organization of Care*, Nancy Folbre and Michael Bittman, eds. New York: Routledge Press, pp. 25–48.

Solberg Eric J., and David C. Wong. 1992. "Family Time Use: Leisure, Home Prod,uction, Market Work, and Work Related Travel." *Journal of Human Resources* 27(3): 485–510.

Sousa-Poza, Alfonso, Hans Schmid, and Rolf Widmer. 2001. "The Allocation and Value of Time Assigned to Housework and Child-Care: An Analysis for Switzerland." *Journal of Population Economics* 14(4): 599–618.

Stewart, Jay. 2008. "The Time Use of Nonworking Men." In *How Do We Spend Our Time? Evidence from the American Time Use Survey*, Jean Kimmel, ed. Kalamazoo, MI: W.E. Upjohn Institute for Employment Research, pp. 109–140.

———. Forthcoming. "The Timing of Maternal Work and Time with Children." *Industrial and Labor Relations Review.*

Strazdins, Lyndall, Mark S. Clements, Rosemary J. Korda, Dorothy H. Broom, and Rennie M. D'Souza. 2006. "Unsociable Work? Nonstandard Work Schedules, Family Relationships, and Children's Well-Being." *Journal of Marriage and Family* 68(2): 394–410.

Strazdins, Lyndall, Rosemary J. Korda, Lynette L-Y Lim, Dorothy H. Broom, and Rennie M. D'Souza. 2004. "Around-the-Clock: Parent Work Schedules and Children's Well-Being in a 24-h Economy." *Social Science and Medicine* 59(7): 1517–1527.

Thomas, Duncan. 1990. "Intra-Household Resource Allocation: An Inferential Approach." *Journal of Human Resources* 25(4): 635–664.

Tunali, Insan. 1986. "A General Structure for Models of Double-Selection and an Application to a Joint Migration/Earnings Process with Remigration." In *Research in Labor Economics, Volume 8, 1986 (Part B), a Research Annual,* R. Ehrenberg, ed. Greenwich, CT: JAI Press, pp. 235–283.

Vanek, Joann. 1974. "Time Spent in Housework." *Scientific American* 231(5): 116–120.

Venn, Danielle. 2004. "Work Timing Arrangements in Australia in the 1990s: Evidence from the Australian Time Use Survey." Unpublished dissertation. Melbourne: University of Melbourne.

Vickery, Clair. 1977. "The Time-Poor: A New Look at Poverty." *Journal of Human Resources* 12(1): 27–48.

Wight, Vanessa R., Sara B. Raley, and Suzanne M. Bianchi. 2008. "Time for Children, One's Spouse, and Oneself among Parents Who Work Nonstandard Hours." *Social Forces* 87(1): 243–271.

Winkler, Anne. 2002. "Measuring Time Use in Households with More Than One Person." *Monthly Labor Review* 125(2): 45–52.

Winston, Gordon. 1982. *The Timing of Economic Activities.* New York: Cambridge University Press.

The Authors

Rachel Connelly is the Bion R. Cram Professor of Economics at Bowdoin College, where she has taught for the last 25 years. Before Bowdoin, Connelly was a graduate student at the University of Michigan and an undergraduate at Brandeis University. Connelly's research has focused on the intersection of economic demography and labor markets, most often on the economics of mothers' employment and child care. Beyond Bowdoin, she has taught at Peking University and Remin University, both in Beijing, and has been a visiting scholar at the U.S. Census Bureau and Peking University Institute of Population Research. She also currently is a research fellow at the Institute for the Study of Labor in Germany.

Jean Kimmel is a professor of economics at Western Michigan University. She is also a research fellow at the Institute for the Study of Labor in Germany. Before joining Western Michigan University's faculty in 2001, she was a senior economist at the W.E. Upjohn Institute for Employment Research from 1989 to 2001. Kimmel earned a BA in economics from George Washington University in 1982, an MA in economics from the University of Delaware in 1984, and a PhD in economics from the University of North Carolina at Chapel Hill in 1990.

Index

The italic letters *f, n,* and *t* following a page number indicate that the subject information of the heading is within a figure, note, or table, respectively, on that page. Double italics indicate multiple but consecutive elements.

About the Institute

The W.E. Upjohn Institute for Employment Research is a nonprofit research organization devoted to finding and promoting solutions to employment-related problems at the national, state, and local levels. It is an activity of the W.E. Upjohn Unemployment Trustee Corporation, which was established in 1932 to administer a fund set aside by Dr. W.E. Upjohn, founder of The Upjohn Company, to seek ways to counteract the loss of employment income during economic downturns.

The Institute is funded largely by income from the W.E. Upjohn Unemployment Trust, supplemented by outside grants, contracts, and sales of publications. Activities of the Institute comprise the following elements: 1) a research program conducted by a resident staff of professional social scientists; 2) a competitive grant program, which expands and complements the internal research program by providing financial support to researchers outside the Institute; 3) a publications program, which provides the major vehicle for disseminating the research of staff and grantees, as well as other selected works in the field; and 4) an Employment Management Services division, which manages most of the publicly funded employment and training programs in the local area.

The broad objectives of the Institute's research, grant, and publication programs are to 1) promote scholarship and experimentation on issues of public and private employment and unemployment policy, and 2) make knowledge and scholarship relevant and useful to policymakers in their pursuit of solutions to employment and unemployment problems.

Current areas of concentration for these programs include causes, consequences, and measures to alleviate unemployment; social insurance and income maintenance programs; compensation; workforce quality; work arrangements; family labor issues; labor-management relations; and regional economic development and local labor markets.